As the Storm Clouds Gathered:

EUROPEAN PERCEPTIONS

OF

AMERICAN FOREIGN POLICY

IN THE 1930s

Howard C. Payne
Raymond Callahan
Edward M. Bennett

MOORE PUBLISHING COMPANY / DURHAM / NORTH CAROLINA

CONTENTS

INTRODUCTION

We have here a volume that is firm in historical scholarship, well written and fascinating to read, and innovative in content and format. It consists of three essays focused on a single significant question: what effect did the perceptions by British, French, and Russian statesmen of United States foreign policy during the interwar years have on the coming of World War II?

Each essay could stand on its own as a model of how the history of diplomatic attitudes should be investigated and presented. Each essay makes its own valuable contribution to the still unresolved problem of the origins of this war. But publishing the essays together in a single volume adds this benefit: the three essays illuminate each other. The alert reader can make comparisons of styles of diplomatic thinking; as in a Henry James novel, by looking at the United States in the mirror of three perceptions he can gain an image of what the United States policies were like, and he can speculate about the might-have-beens of history. To facilitate comparison the authors have inserted an interpretive "perspective" after each article which places the issues in context.

The book thus stimulates thoughtful reflection and inquiry and offers data on which the inquiring mind can work. It should be valuable both to established scholars and to students in this field of diplomatic history.

Harold T. Parker
Professor Emeritus
Duke University

PREFACE

The frightful tragedy of World War II and the shock waves it sent round the globe, whose aftereffects have not even yet subsided, have combined to make the question of its origins one of interest not merely to specialist historians, but to anyone concerned with how the world we live in took on its current shape. One question posed very early in the search for the origins of the Second World War was this: could it all have been averted? Winston Churchill thought the answer clearly was yes, and he argued his case in his own incomparable style in *The Gathering Storm*. Consciously or unconsciously, a generation of historians has been influenced by that brilliant piece of special pleading and has concentrated its attention on the failure of Britain and France to contain Hitler or to achieve the pact with Stalin that might have aided them in doing so.

In this collection of essays the authors have approached the problem from a different point of view. The largest and richest of the western democracies was neither Britain nor France but the United States. A Europe dominated by Hitler would affect the United States as powerfully as, although certainly more slowly than, it would Britain, France, or Russia. The United States was, as Churchill perceived at the time, not only a natural partner but a key factor in any anti-Hitler alliance. Yet, of course, America remained totally aloof. It therefore seemed worthwhile to look at how America appeared from London, Paris, and Moscow to those whose beliefs and interests made them potential opponents of Germany. Were perceptions of the United States a significant factor in the coming of the most terrible of all wars? What follows is a seminal effort to direct attention to a subject much in need of further thought.

Howard C. Payne
Raymond Callahan
Edward M. Bennett

AS THE STORM CLOUDS GATHERED:

European Perceptions of American Foreign Policy in the 1930s

FRENCH SECURITY AND AMERICAN POLICY

IN THE 1930s, A TRIANGULAR DILEMMA

by

Howard C. Payne

At war's end in 1945, amidst Europe's devastation, Joseph Paul-Boncour, onetime premier and diplomat, mused over his recollection of Woodrow Wilson strolling a Paris street in 1919, followed by the "hearts of all the people" in France. How wasteful of the world's chances for a "just and human peace," he reflected, that European politicians and the American people had reduced Wilson to "a King Lear persecuted by his daughters" and thereby thrust Europeans into a twenty-year problem of coping with an isolationist America.[1]

Between two world wars the French experienced more acutely than other nations the ironies of Europe's "American Problem." Not the least irony arose from a certain ambivalence in French statesmen's evaluation of American foreign policy. In the nineteen-twenties they resented, but learned to understand and endure as a fact of life, America's rejection of European political involvements. Yet, among Europeans, the French became the most vulnerable to wishful expectations of a timely American rescue of Europe's peace in the thirties—when "isolationism" in the United States reached its peak.

French ambivalence in the thirties co-existed with, rather than replaced, a diplomatic realism learned from hard experience in 1919 and the early twenties. In those years the French discovered that their prospects of national security against future German resurgence were inextricably woven into a triangular policy dilemma. The dilemma was inherent in France's separate and often tense relations with Great Britain and the United States, and in relationships between the "Anglo-Saxons." French leaders in the thirties strove to change this triangle of differences into a viable entente.

Their problem was more easily defined than solved. However loath to admit it, the French knew that their safety in Europe depended most directly upon Britain's willingness to pledge military aid to France against Germany in case of need, either by an explicit bilateral alliance, or in some kind of collective European security system. Unless the United States were to give something too, at least indirectly, the British withheld such guarantees. But the Americans were unwilling to close the triangle with any significant commitment. So the American problem in French diplomacy barred the way to Anglo-French solidarity, and hence to French security. The dilemma was not of ends but means: how to cast the United States in a third-force European role even though Americans insisted upon playing offstage?

French leaders in the thirties knew they might be courting only failure. Still, wishful hopes of decisive American entry into the European crisis sporadically arose in Paris during most of the period. After Hitler seized power in 1933, France—caught in her triangular dilemma—gradually ran out of imaginable alternatives to American assistance at a time when American policy became ambiguous enough to lure French leaders into grasping at every occasional straw. Here was the climax of a problem which the French had explored during the earlier decade in a way that conditioned their perception of American policy in the thirties.

THE FRENCH "AMERICAN PROBLEM" IN THE TWENTIES

Practical education in the trials of interwar Franco-American relations began at the Paris Peace Conference in 1919 and progressed rapidly thereafter.[2] Convinced that only Germany's permanent "artificial inferiority" (a French expression conceived in all candor) would insure peace, the French sought an extremely punitive treaty. Only when blocked by the first of what they later chose to regard as a series of "Anglo-Saxon" collaborations against French interests, did they yield to pressure and accept a compromise Versailles Treaty. Despite its rigors, the treaty left Germany largely intact in Europe, industrially viable, only provisionally and partly disarmed, and occupied only temporarily along a demilitarized Rhineland. Clearly, Germany retained the potential to rebuild, one day, greater power than could France.

Loss of the Anglo-American Guarantee, 1919

French concessions at Paris implied no abandonment of the "artificial inferiority" idea. They were traded for an Anglo-

4

American promise to help France apply the same policy by other means. In May 1919, the United States, Britain, and France initialed an agreement promising automatic Anglo-American military aid to France in the event of German aggression. Had the treaty lived, the military resources of the three could have held Germany in "artificial inferiority" by the power to deter, much more to repel, a strike against France. But the Anglo-American guarantee died in the United States Senate and thereby released Britain from any obligation to France. When the Americans also rejected the Versailles Treaty—and with it the newborn League of Nations—the French were lonely victors indeed. Services paid for in Paris now would be rendered neither in Washington nor London. France thus entered the twenties with a nagging, triangular policy problem.

From the outset of the abortive guarantee negotiations, the British had made their degree of commitment to France contingent upon American participation. As American policy moved away from internationalism, French leaders had to reassess their security prospects. Their new American problem was flanked by a separate but related British problem. In their subsequent efforts to build a reliable "organization of the peace" (a frequent locution in French diplomatic rhetoric), the French were haunted by the tendency of the one problem repeatedly to abrade the other. Meanwhile their obsession with security led them into actions and attitudes which reduced the possibilities of exploring new ways to close the dislocated triangle.

From Tensions to Detente, 1919-29

"Organization of the peace" after 1919 meant finding substitutes for what the "Anglo-Saxons" had taken away. Literal enforcement of the Versailles Treaty, a fundamental goal, implied a general guarantee of Europe's postwar frontiers, and collection of monetary reparations from Germany. As the French knew, this considerable assignment would require the assistance of other powers in a vigilant European security system armed by pledges to apply collective economic or military sanctions against threats to the status quo. General disarmament must await the creation of such a system; and even then it must stem from criteria compatible with "artificial inferiority" for Germany. Various bilateral and multilateral diplomatic channels could serve these ends. At one time or another, France tried them all. Throughout, her chief direct concern was Britain, and the United States a constant distraction along the sidelines.

Through 1923, Anglo-French relations fared worse than at any time since the century's turn. Repeated French bids for an ironclad bilateral alliance with Britain foundered upon the latter's refusal to guarantee the postwar map of Eastern Europe. For their own security, the British offered a guarantee to the Rhine, but not beyond. In French eyes, such a limited bond seemed no better, if not worse, than none. French attempts to build a small-state alliance network in the East failed to create a reliable power bloc and eroded Britain's will to cooperate on other issues.

Nor did the French succeed in remodeling the League of Nations into a "grand alliance" unequivocally committed to defend the peace. Here again, French initiatives collided with Britain's refusal to generalize her commitments to automatic action in unknown future situations. At this point the outlines of the triangular problem became clearer. Aside from doubts regarding the wisdom of buttressing the existing French predominance on the Continent, the British feared—or professed to fear—the risk of confronting the uncommitted United States in a "collective security" crisis. So long as the Americans, now at naval parity with Britain, owed nothing to the League and freely roamed the seas to trade where they pleased, no British government would accede to French demands. In the words of a French foreign minister,

> If. . .French statesmen allowed themselves usually to be guided by their concern to preserve a close working relationship with Great Britain, whose alliance was indispensable to French security, in their own turn British leaders kept their eyes upon Washington. . . .[3]

As prospects for a European security system faded into the postwar Anglo-French impasse, so did the likelihood of

6

general arms limitation. Disarmament became a chicken-or-the-egg riddle. When the French insisted upon security first, the British argued that arms reduction itself would promote general security. From its official detachment, the United States tended to favor the British. No general disarmament conference became possible until 1932. Meanwhile, though the "Anglo-Saxons" themselves exchanged some heated differences, especially regarding naval limitations, they could combine to denounce French "militarism" and "imperialism" in Europe.

On the related issues of German reparations and inter-allied war debts, triangular differences formed a more complex pattern. The United States opposed heavy reparations on sound economic grounds. Germany could not pay unless she acquired the necessary international exchange through an inconceivably large surplus trade balance. But in the matter of war debts owed by France and Britain, Americans ignored their own economic argument. By coupling an insistence upon full repayment (plus interest) with soaring protective tariffs, they insured that Europeans would suffer unfavorable balances of payments in dealing with the United States. Over Franco-British protests that revision of reparations must be contingent upon revision of war debts, Washington refused all negotiations that might even appear to link the two issues. More than any other irritant in Franco-American relations, the debts generated lasting and mutual resentment. Britain, more tactfully than France, shared the latter's displeasure, but for her own economic interest agreed that reparations must be reduced. This, in turn, increased tensions with France, for whom reparations were less an economic problem than a political means to impose "artificial inferiority" across the Rhine.

Vexed beyond patience by triangular diplomatic frustration and Germany's default on reparations in 1923, France (and Belgium) invaded and occupied the Ruhr industrial region. Though France thus demonstrated to the British that she could act independently in defense of her interests, the Ruhr adventure yielded only negative results. German passive resistance and a total currency inflation aborted French hopes of forcing reparations payments; Anglo-French tensions

7

reached a new high; and Americans were lavish with denunciations. France was internationally isolated with no place to go from the Ruhr but home.

The Ruhr episode ushered France into a detente with Britain and the United States during the later twenties—but for a price. The French had to accept some unwelcome facts of international life. Alone, France could not enforce the peace. Security was an idle dream without British cooperation, limited or not. Nearly thirty years later, Edouard Herriot would end his memoirs with the hard lesson of 1923: "For France, the basis for all action. . .friendship with Great Britain. . . ."[4] And the future of reparations would depend upon American initiative, regardless of French opinion on the justice of war debts and their proper relation to reparations.

Acting upon a British invitation in 1924, the American State Department unofficially stage-managed the adoption of the Dawes Plan, which moved German reparations into a new payments system geared to fluctuations in Germany's ability to pay. This, and the creation of a new German currency, plus the beginning of private dollar loans to the Weimar Republic, was a decisive "Anglo-Saxon" intrusion into French security interests. To be sure, France could now collect reparations, but on a lesser scale and with the risk of further reductions to come. Reparations were no longer a major French political weapon. In effect, German recovery fed upon an American subsidy after 1924—and, as seen from Paris, upon further French sacrifice. For the war debt to the United States was not revised; nor did Washington formally admit any connection between debts and reparations.

In a further aftermath of the Ruhr fiasco, France joined Britain, Germany, and others in the Locarno Pacts of 1925. At Locarno, Germany accepted the Versailles regime in western Europe, including demilitarization of the Rhineland, as final. Britain and Italy guaranteed that acceptance—which was to say, they pledged to fight anyone (including both Germany and France) who might challenge the western status quo by force of arms. Here was at least a limited security system for France; but it was an imperfect achievement. Though Germany agreed to settle differences with her neighbors peaceably, Eastern Europe—her focal area for treaty revisions—lay outside the Anglo-Italian guarantee. The British gave no more than they had considered vital to their own security since 1919. At least, Locarno brought Britain partly to the side of France. At most, it was all that France could expect without American participation.

Shortly before Locarno, the United States had again publicly rejected any role in an international security system and privately warned Britain against the same. In late 1924, hoping to move toward a disarmament conference, the League Assembly drafted the so-called Geneva Protocol, a collective security package proposal open to non-members. The United States promptly declined. Moreover, Secretary of State Hughes confidentially informed the British of his "basic opposition" to the Protocol. If its terms were likely to include Britain in a "proposal of concert against the United States" in a future situation involving American rights, the British should weigh the possible consequences before adhering to the Protocol. American disapproval did not alone cause Britain to veto the proposal; but it reinforced a prior British reluctance to join France in a generalized security pact in Europe or elsewhere. That reluctance continued through the Locarno negotiations where, of course, no one expected an American presence.

Nonetheless, Locarno, the Dawes Plan, and general economic improvement temporarily eased the burden of France's triangular problem. In 1926 the Franco-American debt dispute seemed ended by a formal settlement, primarily on American terms. Two years later, and somewhat to their mutual surprise, France and the United States signed the Kellogg-Briand Agreement to outlaw war as an instrument of national policy. Expanded into the multilateral Pact of Paris, the agreement linked France to Britain and the United States (and many others) in a ratified treaty. More than an empty gesture, the Pact of Paris still fulfilled no one's security needs, much less those of the French. Otherwise the American signature would never have been affixed. It lacked provision for collective enforcement; and it was vitiated by separate national reservations, including those of the United States and Britain. The twenties ended with more triangular good will than political solidarity. Nowhere was this fact better understood than in Paris.

The French View of the American Problem

By 1929, a decade's experience had defined the elements of a security problem whose solution seemed little nearer than in 1919. Until the peace could be "organized" throughout Europe, French security remained in jeopardy. Further British commitment hinged upon an even more unlikely American involvement. To alienate either Britain or the United States was impracticable. Yet any French government which meekly trailed behind separate American and British policies would undercut national interests without hope of tangible gains and arouse certain political opposition within France. A fully independent course, as in 1923, would again recklessly pursue ends that lay beyond available means.

Therefore, French policy-makers in the thirties saw no alternative to attempting the seemingly impossible. They continued to seek solidarity with Britain by bringing the United States into some degree of three-power collaboration by whatever opportunistic means an uncertain future might offer. Appropriately, it was a French historian who later recalled that "the behavior of the United States. . . preoccupied a good part of European public opinion" as the twenties ended.[5]

For many Frenchmen, American behavior after 1919 dissolved a mellowed, romantic image of the United States and created another, born of direct contacts and clashes of interest without precedent before the war. The America of Franklin, Washington, and Jefferson yielded to the harder outlines of Harding, Coolidge, and Hoover. Sentimental memories of a common intellectual heritage and a vaguely continuing alliance—dramatically evoked in 1919 by General Pershing's "Lafayette, we are here"—were rudely erased by Coolidge's summation of the war debts issue: "They hired the money, didn't they?" America the saviour of France and Europe under Wilson had turned into the egoistic beneficiary of Europe's recent sacrifices and seemed bent upon spoiling France's victory in her costliest war. A newer stereotype replaced the old.

10

Those who dealt with the United States shared some of the stereotype, but they also learned not to be so simplistic in evaluating American isolationism. Indeed, the popular French image of "Uncle Shylock" obstructed their own efforts to develop productive Franco-American diplomacy. For French leaders understood that their own people's revised myth of postwar America was matched in the United States by a reciprocal reassessment of France. In the idiom of an ex-ambassador to Washington, the danger was mutual misunderstanding bred by a "conflict of ignorances." Popular resentment, inflamed by the press on both sides, could nullify the efforts of both nations' spokesmen to reach accommodation on contentious issues. France's Washington embassy regularly complained of excessive anti-Americanism in French newspapers. Edouard Herriot, visiting America in 1923, was appalled at the "severely hostile" view of France broadcast most venomously by the Hearst press and echoed in "unjust and cruel words against us" by American senators.[6]

Informed analysts of American policy were caught between two incompatible national interpretations of a shared experience. Though they inclined to ascribe the American version to "an excessive capacity for self-delusion,"[7] they saw the conflicting myths as one fact to identify and face. French leaders perceptibly traced postwar American policy to its prewar wellspring. Americans' overnight conversion to Wilsonian internationalism and their equally abrupt retreat into "isolationism" were consistent with their traditional image of themselves. Aloof from a century of European politics before 1914, Americans had enjoyed the luxury of discerning only the highest moral purpose in their dealings with others. Freedom from formal international engagements cultivated the illusion that free choice was a national birthright. America the moral example offered herself to Europe in 1917; then America of the free hand withdrew the offer when the war was done. Like most of his colleagues, Pierre Flandin (premier and foreign minister in the thirties) understood why Americans believed themselves to be "most equitable and even very generous toward France" during and after the war. Were not the Dawes Plan and loans to Germany, which kept reparations flowing, benefits to a France "swollen with gold,"

11

who persisted in evading just debts?[8] Wishing Europe well, Americans were perplexed to see France sabotage recovery by fomenting tensions throughout the Continent. Why did France, already dominant in Europe, clamor insatiably for more "security" and block a rational approach to disarmament?

In opposition, the French people too were sure of their generosity and good faith, so badly distorted in America. They had fought and bled the most in war, and not for mere self-interest. Again to quote Flandin, they sacrificed "for all that greater collectivity of peoples whose civilization and prosperity were bound up with...political, economic, and social individualism." True, victory required allies. Nonetheless the French "considered themselves their allies' creditors," war debts or not, because they had spent more life, treasure, and resources to win the common victory.[9] They had shared the Wilsonian vision, then were deserted by its author's people. Who more aspired to collective security for all Europeans, then were left alone to pursue it? From within the French self-image, one must conclude that if peace went bankrupt, Americans must blame themselves, along with the British.

From Paris, long before someone applied the term "special relationships" to Anglo-American relations, one could see the "Anglo-Saxons" spontaneously aligning against French interests and hence indirectly playing Germany's game. André Tardieu, disenchanted even with his own countrymen in the early thirties, was an unusually severe but illustrative critic of "Anglo-Saxon" obstructionism. With the United States, Britain intended to share a "domination of the world's transactions" in an updated version of "the old universal dream of the Papacy and Holy Roman Empire." Anglo-American financial and economic nationalism, special favors to Germany in reparations and loans, the crippling of the League and supplementary security proposals—all had smothered a truly international approach to European economic recovery and a solution of the German problem. But when France protested, it was she whom London and Washington accused of "blocking the road to the world's reconstruction."[10]

The often-inflated notion of "Anglo-Saxon" collusion was galling, but French rationality at the diplomatic level concentrated on the real problem. Never a continuing entente, Anglo-American collaboration was a tenuous, *ad hoc* phenomenon. It appeared intermittently in Americans' self-seeking which the British supported because their own interests happened to converge, or which they did not oppose for fear of offending their American cousins. It was this latter, long-range calculation in British policy, a subtle catering to American sensibilities with an eye on the future, that most concerned the French. André de Laboulaye, veteran diplomat and authority on American affairs, thought it

> . . .a fundamental principle of English policy in any international crisis to humor the opinion of the United States. . . .Whether that opinion be that of the government, the Congress, or the public, in the eyes of the English it constitutes an immense force which they desire to conciliate for both the present and future.

He also predicted that the British, even though they knew "that no material support is to be hoped for from the United States in case of a European conflagration," would give Americans "no pretext for refusing their moral support to England." Considered subtly, the French problem was not necessarily to discourage "Anglo-Saxon" cooperation as such. Rather, it was to foster a degree and kind of joint action that would embolden the British to move closer to France and European security. But after a decade of failure in triangular diplomacy, could one realistically anticipate such a new departure?

By 1930 the French found reason for both pessimism and hope. France was no nearer to Britain than Locarno. Explicit, prior commitments to European security could not be expected from across the Atlantic. However, the recent years of prosperity and international detente might soon open new opportunities. American opinion was now less acerbic toward France. Not all Americans were hardbound isolationists; time might win the internationalist minority an audience. The Pact of Paris was a potential framework for closer consultation and, perhaps, even deliberate American cooperation with

Europeans. Skillful persuasion might still cause the United States to facilitate an Anglo-French entente.

Then the thirties began with a spreading world depression. Economic crisis overwhelmed even the United States, thrust unresolved issues of the twenties into another context, and spawned new problems.

DEPRESSION DIPLOMACY AND TRIANGULAR DISUNITY 1930-32

From 1930 until Adolf Hitler became German Chancellor in January 1933, the deepening world economic crisis everywhere intruded into European diplomacy. Old issues joined new stresses in Anglo-French-American relations. French security diplomacy refocused upon immediate dangers and the fleeting tactical possibilities of an international order in rapid disruption. French statesmen anxiously veered this way and that in search of escape from their sense of isolation between Britain and America. Their own vacillation made it more difficult to find a suitable response to the disparity between apparent American intentions and actual American behavior.

Given the integral view of security needs learned in the twenties, the interrelatedness of major European issues in the early thirties predictably drove French diplomacy toward extremes. By 1931 the depression-stricken German Republic, cut off from international loans, was tottering into disaster. Reparations, further revised in 1929 by the Young Plan, were in default. Harried by mushrooming Nazi opposition, Chancellor Bruening called for international aid, further revision of reparations, and the right to join Austria in a customs union. Were France to join a multilateral response to Bruening's pleas, she would risk losing reparations and possibly other treaty provisions in order to shore up an old enemy. The probable alternative, Bruening's defeat and a Nazi takeover, could be even more dangerous. Under Anglo-American pressure to help solve the German crisis, the French saw no reciprocal American willingness to moderate war debts or to admit that general economic distress more than ever demanded a coordinated treatment of debts and reparations.

14

Neither were the British inclined to extend promises beyond Locarno. Should France then yield to the "Anglo-Saxons" and further erode her own security for Germany's sake?

From Paris, the German question reached into the disarmament problem, which in turn probed the core of France's security dilemma. Anticipating the World Disarmament Conference, to begin in 1932, Bruening also demanded "equality" in arms limitation, a principle attractive to the "Anglo-Saxons." Since the latter denied the French thesis that disarmament was conceivable only within a viable European security structure, any direct arms reduction founded upon "equality" meant the end of Germany's "artificial inferiority." France alone was expected to sacrifice vital national interests for Germany's rehabilitation.

An Illusory "Consultative Pact"

Scanning for openings across the Atlantic, the French saw a possible way out through Washington and into a "consultative pact" among France, Britain, and the United States. America need give no explicit commitments to the future. The pact would somehow combine a declaration of moral solidarity, cooperation in mutual depression problems, and the promise immediately to confer if peace were imperilled. Paris would then trade cooperation in the German crisis for American recognition of debts and reparations as integrated issues, and "equality" in disarmament for British participation in a European security agreement.

Off and on for three years, French officials considered many variants of the "consultative" springboard to security. One version, offered by René Massigli, chief delegate to the Disarmament Conference in 1932, reflected the typical mixture of realistic appraisal and wishful thinking which nourished the consultative idea. Massigli argued that all experience since 1919—particularly the stillborn Geneva Protocol of 1924—proved that no integral, universal "organization of the peace" was feasible. France must accept "the profound repugnance of the American government to undertake any long-range engagements which draw it into European complications. . . ." It followed that Britain would out of "necessity" refuse commitments "whose execution would risk

15

bringing her into conflict with the United States." Indeed, said Massigli, were even Locarno to be renegotiated, the British would drop out because of their Dominions' reluctance and persistent American isolationism. Therefore, France must seek security in segments, at different levels of commitment.

Massigli's plan called first for a multilateral "consultative pact" binding only to the unpredictable degree "determined by the necessity to obtain the American signature." No British government could refuse such an affiliation with the United States. To launch the plan, France must cultivate those Americans who believed that the Pact of Paris implied an obligation of mutual consultation. Let that obligation be spelled out on paper to say that any breach of the Pact would be judged a violation against all signatories, who would immediately concert to mobilize world opinion as a moral sanction and to discuss other peace-keeping options. Those states willing to apply either an arms or economic embargo might then proceed without hindrance by others who chose not to do so. This would remove the British fear of colliding with the United States (who would never promise sanctions in advance) when acting in concert to uphold League of Nations principles. Hence Britain could safely enter a binding "European Regional Accord" to enforce peace.

We may look back in wonder at the French dream of arriving at security through an American consultative pledge, when so many adverse signs were posted along the way. Still, without venturing to ask if Britain would have played her assigned role, we can see why the French did find a shred of hope. Expecting little, they dared ask very little: only a promise to talk, without further strings, and a covenant to *refrain from opposing* other states' concerted measures to deter lawbreakers. As for war debts and reparations, the French reasoned that the depression, in its perverse way, ought to recall Americans to international responsibility. Now a fallen economic giant, the United States out of self-interest would try to rise again through a collective approach to depression problems. Then, creative diplomacy could change the debts and reparations deadlock into compromise on the German question and a gateway into a comprehensive economic recovery program.

16

The French "Stimson Cult"

Such expectations were nurtured by a persistent belief that Henry L. Stimson, Hoover's Secretary of State until early 1933, could lead his nation into a new venture in international leadership. The French considered Stimson—as he himself later put it—an aspirant "honest broker" bent upon helping Europeans settle their differences and teaching Americans to focus their moral influence in support of world stability. On the French checklist of vital issues, Stimson scored consistently high. He admitted the inseparability of debts and reparations and preferred to liquidate both. He understood that "equality" in disarmament, without inclusive security guarantees, would only mask German rearmament. It was he who insisted that the Pact of Paris called for regular, even institutionalized, consultation among its members. Stimson's professed hope was to become the catalyst in a fusion of Anglo-French efforts to administer peace. At the London Naval Conference in 1930 he suggested that if Britain were to expand her security commitments to France, the United States would then consider a consultative pact. Though Hoover repudiated the London overture, Stimson continued to skirt the same sensitive theme during visits to European capitals in 1931-32.

Concurrently, during the Manchurian crisis, when Stimson's incipient alignment with the League faded into the "Hoover-Stimson Doctrine" of non-recognition and non-intervention in Japanese conquest, Europeans saw that Hoover had again pulled the reins on the Secretary. But perhaps a continuing need for European support of American Far Eastern interests and economic diplomacy would increase Stimson's determination to lead Europe toward security.

Until late 1932 a French "Stimson cult" flourished in Paris and Washington. Ambassador Paul Claudel, renowned lyric poet and career diplomat, advised Paris to take its cue from Stimson's assertion that "a close and confident entente among the three great democratic powers" could and must evolve. Jules Henry, Claudel's chargé, also expected Stimson to change "the orientation of American policy toward closer cooperation with Europe" by developing a new "American doctrine of consultation." Henry knew that though Stimson

17

could not deliver an ironclad commitment, no major power could afford to ignore American opinion. Were that opinion to align in no more than moral solidarity with those who strove for peace, "the action of America [could] be of capital importance" in deterring troublemakers. Stimson must "manage" American opinion by teaching the difference between a "pact of security or guarantee and the practice of consultation." Because consultation was imbedded in "Anglo-Saxon" domestic custom, Henry believed that Americans might learn to elevate it to "the force of law" in international politics.

As the Hoover administration neared its end after November 1932, Premier Edouard Herriot risked his political future upon an attempt to resume war debt payments and to accept German "equality" in disarmament—in exchange for an American consultative pledge. Inspired by Stimson's public statements, the so-called Herriot Plan envisaged an elaborate security organization in three "concentric circles." An outer "consultative" circle would include the United States and other Pact of Paris members. A middle circle of League members would enclose an inner group, including Britain, joined in a European mutual assistance treaty. The sides of France's problem triangle would, in effect, be connected. And a relative disarmament could safely be undertaken. But, of course, this happy ending was not to be.

French hopes in late 1932 subsisted upon a refusal to accept the preceding three years' lessons as final. Stimson never was in a position to become Europe's Messiah, hemmed in as he was by isolationist opinion, a President acutely sensitive to that opinion, and his own reservations as to involvement in Europe. Devoted to the idea of consultation, and a dedicated "honest broker," Stimson knew his inability to extend his government's engagements abroad. Consistently, he explained to Europeans, and for a last time to Paul Claudel in October 1932, that he could do no more than urge Europeans first to agree among themselves. Then, later on, the United States would offer concurrence "by words and deed" in lieu of a prior written agreement which, anyway, was "politically impossible" to exact from an unwilling public and Congress. Only European initiative could activate American collaboration.

Stimson's situation paralleled that of his French counterparts. To win Britain to a security pact the French needed an American consultative pledge; but he could offer only the possibility of an undefined American cooperation after an Anglo-French understanding. And he doubted that between themselves either France or Britain would concede enough to become effective partners. The locution "politically impossible," as a rationale for inaction, also described attitudes in Paris and London. This Stimson learned in an illustrative encounter with Premier Pierre Laval in October 1931. Parrying Stimson's suggestion that a revision of the "artificial inferiority" policy toward Germany might produce closer Anglo-French relations, Laval replied that any concession which his people interpreted as a treaty revision was "politically impossible" for at least the next decade. When Laval then asked for a consultative pact, it was Hoover's turn to veto the proposal as a "political impossibility." Stimson sketched more than his own situation when he later recalled the early thirties:

> ...all the major powers by 1931 had entrenched themselves in self-righteous attitudes which pointed the finger of responsibility at someone else. . . .More than that, the cooler statesmen of each nation knew what concession, in abstract fairness, their own countries should make. Only they knew too—or thought they knew—that these concessions were "political impossibilities."[11]

A Clash of Political Impossibilities, 1931-32

"Political impossibilities" so stultified relations among the three major democracies after 1930 that one wonders now how the French kept alive their expectations of a consultative pact until Herriot's abortive plan in late 1932. In 1930 France refused to join the "Anglo-Saxons" in the London Naval Treaty. In 1931 she played the villain in British and American eyes by delaying action on the German crisis until it was too late. French financial maneuvers wrecked the Austro-German Customs Union and the credit system of Central Europe, and accelerated an international chain reaction that forced Britain

19

off the gold standard. All along, French strategy was to force the United States to concede the linkage of debts and reparations. When Laval did exact President Hoover's half-promise to revise debts along with reparations, Congress promptly annulled the French victory. The German Republic was wounded beyond recovery, triangular relations grew brittle under multiple strains, and reparations had to be virtually cancelled by a 90 per cent cut at Lausanne in June 1932.

Even the belated French concession at Lausanne was faulted by a tactic to split the "Anglo-Saxons" and bring the Americans to heel once more on the debts issue. A common Anglo-French interest was clear: if Germany were to be relieved of reparations, why should the United States collect in full? By a so-called "Gentleman's Agreement," Britain joined France in withholding ratification of the Lausanne Agreement until the Americans reconsidered war debts. Following through, the French obtained a tenuous consultative agreement with Britain which had little substance beyond a mutual promise to continue the search for a disarmament formula and to attend a world economic conference in 1933.

In the United States, a public furor mounted against France, whose politicians and press responded in kind. From Washington, Claudel surveyed coast-to-coast outrage against his country's "sinister designs," allegedly ranging from conspiracy to hold Germany and Europe in misery, to an attack on the American dollar. Jules Henry judged that American francophobia, endemic since the early twenties, was now "especially profound." He urged his government to manipulate the French press into a "polemical truce" because "the Americans, despite their somewhat uncouth demeanor," were "more sensitive than anyone to the attentions others pay them."

Seeking to calm the storm, French leaders bewailed the magnified "political impossibility" now certain to face Stimson and other American internationalists in a deteriorating situation which French diplomacy had helped to precipitate. French statesmen could rationalize their obsessive behavior on the debt issue by reiterating the "political impossibility" of defying French opinion in such a passionate matter—an opinion which they themselves had fanned to greater heat in 1931 and 1932. Ever wishing to draw America closer, they ended by pushing her away.

Even such pro-Americans as Paul Claudel and Edouard Herriot shared their countrymen's fury on the debt issue to the point of harboring a self-defeating ambivalence in evaluating American policy and its possibilities for France. Solicitous of American sensibilities on one hand, they were chronically tempted to teach Americans a lesson on the other. Claudel, for instance, was a highly perceptive and sympathetic analyst of American society and politics, subtly aware of the nuances in Americans' image of themselves and others. An admirer of Stimson, he frequently cautioned Paris against words or actions apt to provoke anti-French sentiment and hence further to tie the Secretary's hands. After the Lausanne Agreement, he warned that "a premature action or even simple reckless language could produce, in the present uncertainty, irreparable results." Yet Claudel was momentarily elated with the thought that Lausanne thrust the United States "directly into the face of her responsibilities" and formed the nucleus of a coalition that would force the Americans to acknowledge Europe's "refusal to be dictated to." Herriot, even while gambling his premiership in order to draw the United States into his "concentric circles" of security, privately shared Claudel's rancor. "In France," he told some British diplomats, "we are disgusted with American cynicism."

The War Debts Crisis of December 1932

Herriot and his advisers acknowledged that legally and morally—and for diplomatic expediency—France must pay her next installment on the debt on December 15. They soon learned what "political impossibility" could mean in France. Herriot failed to convince parliament, which resoundingly vetoed the payment. To Americans, France in default looked all the worse alongside Britain, who rejected a French bid for a common default. Soon out of office, Herriot was left amidst the wreckage of his security plan to brood over the implications of a cartoon in *Life*, the American newsmagazine,

21

which depicted France as a comely woman dancing, hands over heart, upon heaps of gold above a legend taken from a popular American song: "I can't give you anything but love."

A month later, Adolf Hitler began the Nazification of Germany. Security, not war debts, thereafter was the French government's prime concern, though the two problems remained perversely interrelated for years. Long afterward, Paul Reynaud was still convinced that "the bitterness left in American hearts by this affair of the debts" crystallized American determination to abandon Europe in the later thirties.[12]

We could turn Reynaud's thesis around to help explain French intransigence in December 1932, a time when bitterness was a two-way street. The "affair of the debts" reflected a widespread belief that the United States had already abandoned Europe at the Disarmament Conference, Stimson notwithstanding. Insisting upon security before disarmament, the French saw themselves beleaguered by the "Anglo-Saxons" and Germany. Their chances of integrating arms limitation with security guarantees depended upon American cooperation, which Herriot and some others hoped to win by acceding to Washington's hard line on war debts. Instead, they got the Hoover Plan of June 1932—a proposal for across-the-board arms reduction without reference to a consultative agreement or security needs. They saw the British, privately critical of Hoover's scheme, support it anyway, fearing—Paul-Boncour surmised—"not to be in accord with the United States."[13] Though France finally yielded on "equality" in November, contingent upon security arrangements, Albert Sarraut later recalled, "we had ceaselessly to defend ourselves against the accusation of militarism or imperialism coming from England or the United States. . . ."[14]

Also in November, Hoover's electoral defeat swept away the Stimson image. Thus by December, the French parliament's mood matched that of André Tardieu, who blamed Americans for the failure of French disarmament plans. Their pretended cooperation at Geneva, Tardieu charged, was "merely verbal when it is a question of constituting an effective guarantee of security," and hence a

22

service only to Germany.[15] Nine years after the Ruhr, the default of 1932 was a far weaker show of French independence for the purpose of rebuking a more elusive adversary.

RENEWED HOPES AND AMBIGUOUS RAPPROCHEMENT
1933-34

As 1933 began, where could French diplomacy go? The debt crisis was a sobering experience. Joseph Paul-Boncour, foreign minister in four cabinets from December 1932 to February 1934, deplored the outburst against "Uncle Shylock." Though he thought Herriot "fell nobly," France was the loser. With Hitler in charge at Berlin, Paul-Boncour knew that the triangular game must be played in earnest. To save the peace, France and Britain needed the United States as badly as in 1917.[16] But Franco-American relations were never worse. Another debt payment was due in June. Deadlock ruled the Disarmament Conference, where no security possibilities were in sight. The depression had invaded France late, but decisively, during 1932. World recovery was now a vital national interest. France's major problems continued to impel her toward Washington.

It was time to begin again, though the omens were negative. Paul Claudel expected a field day for anti-French extremists in the Senate and throughout America. Among "the extremely grave consequences" of the recent debt default, Claudel counted "nearly incalculable" moral damage, probable boycotts of French goods and services, and a vindictive American policy to come. Pro-French Americans were "plunged into consternation" and the "patient work of many years. . .ruined at one blow." Claudel and Herriot did find a thread or two of hope. France's December "thunderbolt" might speed Americans' "education" and make them seek "a complete and immediate solution" of the debts issue. One could only hope that cooler heads in Congress and the government would not forget that only cooperation with France and Britain could ease the depression in America. Economic necessity, then, might lead to wider collaboration

23

in the direction of European security.

New Optimism: From Stimson to Roosevelt,
November 1932 to February 1933

Claudel's concern for the future reawakened an almost nostalgic appreciation of the constraints which had plagued Stimson and Hoover. Just after the American election, Claudel had reported: "M. Hoover has perished" because of "the entire country's condemnation" of Republican "isolation and megalomania. One can hope that a spirit of liberalism will replace a selfish and shabby conservatism." But after the December crisis, he reflected that Hoover had really desired "to go as far as possible to meet the desires of France," even to the verge of resuming "the broad policy of Wilson." The hapless President knew that isolationism was obsolete; but he was "harassed by his party's policy and the hostility of Congress." No wonder that Stimson was limited to "sporadic, indirect, and awkward initiatives, followed by immediate rebuffs that did more harm than good." Until Franklin D. Roosevelt took office in March 1933, the French could only hope that the new President would more successfully pursue Stimson's frustrated aims. Meanwhile, Claudel reminded Paris never to forget that "an entente with America, leading to another with England, is the indispensable condition of world recovery."[1][7]

In January, Premier Paul-Boncour very confidentially began to woo Roosevelt. He instructed Claudel to probe the President-Elect's views by "judiciously posed questions" and to assure him that the French government accepted the legality of its debt, even though an incorrigible public opinion did not. Were some "new gesture" to come from America, France would seek a compromise on the debt within a wider economic understanding.

Scarcely had Claudel begun his overture when Roosevelt himself astonished the French with an initiative which turned dejection into euphoria and launched a Roosevelt cult that outshone the earlier Stimson image. In late January, William C. Bullitt appeared unannounced before Paul-Boncour as Roosevelt's confidential emissary. He requested that the Premier send a trusted agent to meet the President-Elect in

24

New York for a frank discussion of the debts issue. Moreover, Bullitt declared, Roosevelt intended to include in his inaugural address a strong reassertion of Franco-American amity. In "very clear contrast" with Hoover, Roosevelt would propose negotiations, in hopes of making the French parliament more disposed to reconsider its recent action.

After a brief, incredulous delay to verify Bullitt's status, Paul-Boncour cultivated his diplomatic windfall, guided closely by Claudel's continual advice. Through a flurry of "very secret" despatches between the two, one can trace a Franco-American rapprochement and a French reassessment of American policy. Paul-Boncour sent Emmanuel Monick, Claudel's financial attaché, to confer with Roosevelt on February 17. Monick found the President-Elect less preoccupied with the French debt than with the entire international economic crisis. Roosevelt, in Monick's words, saw no solution "unless an effective collaboration be established in the immediate future among the United States, France, and England." Assuring Monick that France must be included in forthcoming economic talks with Britain, Roosevelt insisted that "the interests of France. . .are so close to those of the United States. . .that your place is at our sides. . . ." Claudel enthusiastically referred to "this new entente between France and America" as "the essential direction" of Roosevelt's future policy.

Spurred by the Ambassador's optimism, French leaders raised their expectations of a diplomatic breakthrough. After talking with Roosevelt and Cordell Hull, soon to become Secretary of State, Claudel advised Paris to deal directly "on the important questions" with the former instead of Hull, who lacked his chief's warmth and personal understanding of France. Claudel sensed and reported Roosevelt's absolute agreement with the French thesis that international security and economic salvation required an effective triangular entente to create "a worldwide organization of peace."

How far would Roosevelt go? At the very most, Claudel thought he might one day resume the path of Wilson, though his intellect, personality, and methods were utterly different. A pragmatist, warmly personal in his public style, and endowed with "incomparable popularity," Roosevelt was master of an unorthodox "barn-storming" political technique that could sway Americans. At the least, Claudel predicted, the new President would outstrip Stimson and Hoover in pursuit of a consultative pact, cooperative progress in disarmament, and strong leadership in the World Economic Conference later in 1933. But even Roosevelt was not "ripe" for involvement in international arms control or a European security system. Nonetheless, the mere phenomenon of American-British-French entente upon fundamentals would reassure the world, deter aggression, foster an Anglo-French security agreement, and promote economic rehabilitation.

In Paris hopes arose that an entente on the debts issue might well escalate into something more comprehensive. Roosevelt seemed to agree that the first step to a new Franco-American agenda must be to overcome the fiasco of the previous December. On this perennial dispute, a position paper by Jacques Lyon, financial and commercial expert in the foreign ministry, reflected the positive reports from Washington. Lyon considered Roosevelt's invitation to tripartite negotiations on the debts an incomparable chance for France to counter the Americans' habitual favoritism toward Britain. A byproduct of compromise on the debts might be "a preliminary entente of the three powers," with France playing arbiter between the "Anglo-Saxons" in order to insure success at the long-awaited World Economic Conference. And from there, perhaps the road would broaden into "a general entente of the three great liberal powers. . .for the defense of liberty" against the dictators. Lyon argued that the foundation of Franco-American rapprochement was Roosevelt's sense of American self-interest, rather than altruism or sentimental regard for France. His progress against the depression at home absolutely required cooperation with France and Britain. And his apparent predilection toward gathering many problems into one diplomatic complex offered a rare opportunity for France to exploit.

Faith in Roosevelt soared until after his inaugural in March. Ambassador Claudel willingly transferred to Brussels to make way for André de Laboulaye, an oldtime friend of the Roosevelts. In April, Paul-Boncour (now foreign minister for Edouard Daladier) sent Herriot on a special mission to cultivate the new President and certain Senators. Both Laboulaye and Herriot reconfirmed Claudel's earlier impressions and heard Roosevelt express his "wishes to make an effort for a universal organization of the peace." No phrasing could have been dearer to the French.

Promises Become Frustration, March-October 1933

By late spring, the time for presidential generalities was over and the moment for action at hand, particularly in the continuing Disarmament Conference at Geneva, and in London, where the World Economic Conference convened in June. On May 19, Roosevelt's image glowed in both cities when he promised the two conferences a significant degree of American cooperation. In disarmament, the United States favored a British compromise plan which included a consultative agreement and non-aggression pact. To the French this suggested an American breakthrough into comprehension of the vital relationship between security and arms reductions. If so, they could also support the British plan. Roosevelt's references to forthcoming economic diplomacy were equally promising. Assurance of real American participation was implicit in his concluding statement:

> . . .if any strong nation refuses to join. . .in these concerted efforts for political and economic peace, the one at Geneva and the other at London, progress can be obstructed and ultimately blocked. . .I urge that no nation assume such a responsibility and that all. . .translate their professed policies into action.

In Geneva the Disarmament Conference paused to await the outcome at London.

During preparatory negotiations for the Economic Conference, the French had at first tried to align solidly with Britain on the debts problem and to attain triangular agreement that mutual currency stabilization take priority on the agenda. Their failure in the first effort did not inhibit their willingness to compromise for the sake of a three-power monetary agreement designed to become the foundation of an international concert against the depression. Never had French financial diplomacy shown such flexibility. But the Conference failed when Roosevelt, piqued by what he chose to regard as an Anglo-French coalition against him, and only vaguely cognizant of the financial intricacies involved, suddenly rejected currency stabilization.[18]

Roosevelt's America seemed to be reverting to an erratic fluctuation between internationalism and parochial nationalism reminiscent of the Hoover-Stimson era. At Geneva, French hopes received another blow in October, when Hitler announced Germany's withdrawal from both the Disarmament Conference and the League, on the very day France yielded to the United States and Britain on the "equality" principle. Louis Barthou, Paul-Boncour's successor at the foreign ministry, revived a familiar French lament to summarize the first year's experience with Rooseveltian diplomacy in contrast with the presidential image: "it is always France who is called upon to make the sacrifices."

Roosevelt Revised, 1934

Disappointment in London and Geneva, and the Nazi specter in Berlin, led the French to re-examine the Roosevelt image. By 1934, other unsolved problems paled beside the compelling need for security. While Louis Barthou resumed a hard line on disarmament and tried to conjure up an eastern security bloc, Ambassador Laboulaye and others studied a Roosevelt whose earlier neo-Wilsonian profile dissolved into the more complex, enigmatic face of an unpredictable human being. He was caught like Stimson in domestic politics, ambivalent as Hoover regarding the relative priorities of international conciliation and immediate national interests, and given to puzzling vacillations. At once artful and sincere toward Europeans, the revised Roosevelt alternated verbal encouragement with recurrent procrastination in deeds. Laboulaye, who among Frenchmen probably knew the President best, discerned "above all an empiricist," without doctrine or consistent plans. An idea picked up with genuine enthusiasm today might be discarded tomorrow, especially for domestic political expediency.

What French leaders feared most—a resurgence of American

28

isolationism—was undoubtedly occurring in late 1933. They had expected Roosevelt's charisma, working upon public hopes for the success of his New Deal, to carry his internationalism along. But as early as June 1933, Laboulaye predicted correctly that if things went badly at Geneva and the Economic Conference, a swell of negative American opinion would sweep the President with it. Despite his "generous and cosmopolitan spirit," Roosevelt was "no less sensitive to criticism" than other Americans. And Laboulaye observed much new criticism in the American press and Congress at a time when Roosevelt was showing disappointment at Europeans' failure to respond more energetically to his moral inspiration. The French press abetted the renewal of isolationism by distorting the New Deal and carping at its leader. Once again, Laboulaye feared, the two peoples' conflicting images of themselves and one another would in the end cost both dearly. Laboulaye was obviously shaken by such American press headlines as: "France Demands That the United States Abandon Its Neutrality."

During 1934, gloom continued to vie with lingering faith in Roosevelt. Nothing filled the vacuum left by the abortive Economic Conference. Disarmament became a lost cause, and with it the French dream of a built-in security system. There were American reassurances aplenty, all significantly abstract and open-ended. Through Norman Davis, his representative, Roosevelt vowed that he wished to help France find a solution "by every means in his powers," but was unable to suggest the means. Instead, Davis posed a question: why could not Europeans initiate a "general accord" on disarmament and related "regional arrangements necessary in Europe?" France must understand that American policy was cooperative, but it would not press anyone to accept any particular solution. American policy, as seen from Paris, seemed to have retrogressed to that of Stimson in his talk with Claudel in October 1932: let Europe make the first move, then the President would see what he could do. From his new post in Brussels, Paul Claudel blamed his countrymen as much as the Americans for degrading the intent of "a great man." He found the results "enough to make one cry."[19]

Claudel referred especially to war debts, the incurable

sickness in Franco-American relations. After December 1932 the French parliament refused to pay until major concessions came from America, whose Congress and people were equally determined to reject cancellation or revision. In 1934 no issue caused Laboulaye more agony than this "near tragic" misunderstanding, just when France needed "any of the cards which we could and must have in our hand for the future." Laboulaye, Herriot, Barthou and others in Paris counted upon Roosevelt still to bypass debts and get on to larger depression issues, such as currency stabilization. But the President, like the French government itself, had to face his own "political impossibility." Early in April the Congress, without serious opposition, voted the Johnson Act, which forbade even private loans to countries in default on war debts. Laboulaye was certain that Roosevelt, no friend of the Act, would use its loopholes to avoid declaring France again in default if the French Chamber would appease Congress by authorizing even a token payment on the next due date in June. In return, Roosevelt would at a later, more propitious time, reopen negotiation on the total debt.

Laboulaye's optimism was unjustified. In a stormy meeting on May 10, 1934 the French Council of Ministers backed down before its own "political impossibility" and refused to ask parliament for a payment on the debt. Again, Herriot was outvoted. Neither his quoting of Laboulaye's urgent warnings, nor his emotional reminders of American aid in 1917, nor even his plea that French security hung upon the decision, could overcome the opposition. To Herriot's bitter chagrin, France would continue "its role of dishonest debtor."[20] When the latest French default became official on June 15, Roosevelt conveyed his assurance that at some indefinite time, but certainly not before the next Congressional elections, he would strive to reduce the French debt. The embassy related this news to Paris without comment. The French were learning to live with the President's blending good will with inaction.

Thereafter, Laboulaye's prediction of the previous year became an axiom in Paris: Roosevelt could risk international gestures "of an entirely moral character"; but, Laboulaye was sure that he would never dare advocate any "precise obligation for the future." Nevertheless, as the European crisis intensified after 1934, the French had little acceptable choice but to convince themselves that even Roosevelt's moral support might be decisive, "even the determinant in case of a threat of war." Although the Roosevelt cult had lost its glitter, its essence lived off of the difficult times ahead.

GRASPING AT STRAWS, 1935-38

From March 1935, when Hitler tore the German disarmament pages from the Versailles Treaty, until the Munich Pact of 1938, the French lived in a series of overlapping domestic and foreign crises. Gradually, they exhausted all foreign policy options except to follow Britain in an attempt to "appease" totalitarian appetites that would not be appeased. One by one, the conditions of Germany's "artificial inferiority" crumbled. German rearmament, the Ethiopian and Rhineland crises of 1935-1936, and the Spanish Civil War reduced Versailles, Locarno, the League, the Pact of Paris, and France's small-state alliance system to ruins.

Without allies who would or could resist, France remained captive to her triangular dilemma. She had no choice but to seek and maintain a close Anglo-French entente, now available if France would assist an appeasement policy that undermined the vestiges of security. Unless, of course, the United States were to intervene with an alternative. Late in 1936, William C. Bullitt, recently named Ambassador in Paris, wrote directly to Roosevelt: "I have never encountered such complete hopelessness." Yet he could add that the French still prayed for Roosevelt to become "the miracle man" in Europe.[21]

The Prospects For American Moral Support
Awaiting each crisis in its turn, French leaders grasped at even the most limited offer of Roosevelt's "moral support." Seldom did anyone again expect a real entente. Having plumbed the depth of American isolationism—most overtly symbolized by the Johnson Act and the Neutrality Law of 1935—the French, to retain hope at all, had to separate Roosevelt from his people in their thinking. Instead of

ambiguity and indecision in the President's mind, the French preferred to see a convinced internationalist unwillingly restrained. Rather than a skeptic of Europeans' ability to capitalize upon American moral support even if offered, they saw a political tactician awaiting the moment when the European crisis became frightful enough to awaken domestic support for his timely mediation of European peace. Resignation could thus coexist with hope.

Laboulaye reported that most Americans wanted "peace at any price"—for themselves. Even so, he recalled how "unforeseen events" in Europe had changed Wilson and given him the backing of a once aloof nation. Might not new "unforeseen events" also free Roosevelt? Paul Reynaud rekindled his faith in the President during a visit in 1936 and left Washington regretting only that Roosevelt "has against him the Babbitts" of America.[22] Yvon Delbos, foreign minister from 1936 to 1938, rejoiced at Roosevelt's large electoral victory in 1936, because of "the President's personal dispositions in favor of France and his spirited personal desire. . .despite the resistance he meets in Congress and public opinion, to cooperate in every possible degree" with efforts for peace.

When French observers looked away from Roosevelt to assess his domestic political environment, the view became completely somber. Jules Henry, attaché in Washington, in a lengthy analysis for Delbos, traced the American people's retreat during the depression years into an "impregnable fortress" of isolationism. He found that even while rejecting Wilson and the League, Americans had not chosen complete isolationism in the twenties. But unfortunately, certain sources of hostility toward France and disenchantment with Europeans' ability to help themselves gradually accumulated. Disarmament negotiations became interminable, petty, and haggling. Above all, the war debts and reparations disputes bred francophobia.

Henry placed the real onset of isolationism between 1930 and 1934. The depression years inflamed old grievances and turned Americans inward upon themselves as never before. In their repudiation of Stimson, Americans showed their "overly simplistic" approach to "the complexity of European

32

problems." They never understood that without security first, disarmament was an illusion. They reacted passionately against the Lausanne "Gentleman's Agreement" and the French default of 1932. Concurrently, a desperate obsession with their economic failure completed Americans' submission to the world's worst case of international myopia. Roosevelt's sincere internationalist impulse of 1933, like Stimson's before it, necessarily remained only verbal. Indeed, the inability of Europeans themselves to counter the Nazi menace may have convinced even Roosevelt that inaction was the better policy anyway. Without some European initiative to indicate a sense of common self-preservation, Henry concluded, France would "in vain" anticipate a change in American policy.

Further, Henry implied, without bringing himself to say so, that even to depend upon "moral support" might be illusory. In the twenties, when there was no need, "a simple declaration by the president of the United States literally would have sufficed" to keep the peace. Now, when the need was urgent, some Europeans believed that only America's onetime economic might had made her so imposing. Iconoclastic leaders in Japan, Italy, and Germany were "less and less impressed by the Platonic communiqués and declarations of the government in Washington." So, Henry advised, "we are reduced to asking ourselves what would be the Americans' role on the day when war broke out." The answer seemed clear: Americans would stand aside, though they would "eventually pay very dearly for their neutrality."

The next three years confirmed Jules Henry's assessment. If one were to ask why the present study devotes so few pages to Franco-American security diplomacy in the late thirties, the answer would be that there was so little to narrate. French efforts to relate the United States to European crisis were sporadic and unproductive. But they continued, because occasional American gambits allowed the Roosevelt image a flickering life.

Overlapping Crises, 1935-1937

In the Italo-Ethiopian crisis of 1935-1936, American "moral support" showed its inadequacy. Indeed, the Anglo-French appeasement of Mussolini as a potential ally against the greater German threat actually counted upon American isolationism. Both the British and French governments defended their application of only meaningless sanctions against Italy by pointing to the impossibility of stronger measures without American participation. Advocates of strong sanctions looked to Roosevelt for leadership; the appeasers counted upon American abstention as the key to holding Mussolini's friendship. Both groups miscalculated. Roosevelt's personal appeal to Mussolini and Hull's ineffective "moral embargo" on oil sales to Italy paraded the weakness of "moral intervention" in Europe. And Anglo-French hypocrisy, Léon Blum pointed out, merely confirmed American isolationists' bias against the cynicism of European politics.[23]

Moreover, the Ethiopian affair stimulated Congress to tighten the Neutrality Act of 1935. A new law in early 1936 left the President no leeway in denying war materials to both aggressor and victim in an armed conflict, and compelled him to withhold arms even from states acting against aggression through the League or to defend the Pact of Paris. Still, Laboulaye noted Roosevelt's personal opposition to this neutrality policy, without dwelling upon the latter's inability to prevent it. Thus he could believe that Roosevelt sought a proper time and means to "orient American policy in the direction of...the democratic countries and to ours in particular." The time, but not the way, was soon at hand.

In March 1936, Hitler compounded the Ethiopian crisis by remilitarizing the German Rhineland in defiance of Versailles, Locarno, and the League. Four months later the outbreak of civil war in Spain provided a theater for Italo-German intervention on behalf of the anti-republican forces. In the Rhineland, French defeatism and British appeasement gave Hitler his victory. In Spain, a farcical Anglo-French sponsorship of a general "non-intervention" agreement did not deter the Axis powers from assisting the Republic's eventual death. If ever the French needed American intervention, it was during 1936.

Before the Rhineland crisis, Roosevelt began the year by publicly denouncing the dictators' reversion to the "law of the sword." In Berlin, Ambassador Dodd went much farther by warning Hitler's foreign minister that a violation of

Locarno would incite a "scandalized public opinion" in the United States to support "the strictest economic sanctions." Germany would then be "boycotted by the whole world." Dodd interpreted the President's statement in similar, though less dramatic terms, for André François-Poncet, French ambassador to Germany. But the latter predicted that despite the Germans' irritation at Roosevelt's "quasi-Wilsonian pretension," they could count as before upon his "rigorous neutrality" in a real crisis.

Events quickly proved François-Poncet correct. Two days after Hitler's troops moved, Pierre Flandin—desperate for lack of British support—begged the American ambassador to implore Roosevelt publicly to condemn the Rhineland action. Flandin hoped such a declaration would goad the British into supporting France more than he expected it to deter Hitler! Hull, not Roosevelt, replied through embassy channels: although he "thoroughly" understood and sympathized with the French request, he could only reply that "we do not feel that we could appropriately make any comment at this time." To Roosevelt, Hull explained that though the Germans clearly violated Versailles and Locarno, the American-German peace agreement of 1921 remained unaffected.[24]

In Washington, Laboulaye admitted that Roosevelt's "complete reserve" mirrored the nation's overwhelming intention to remain aloof. Morally, America sided with France. Hull was "profoundly shocked" and State Department personnel showed "a certain shame." Otherwise, France could expect nothing. The arch-isolationist Senator Borah said he was glad to see the "abolition" of Versailles. Worse, even Eleanor Roosevelt expressed similar views in her syndicated newspaper column. Flandin had little left to say to Americans regarding the Rhineland.

Yvon Delbos, Flandin's successor, fared no better during the Spanish conflict. Hull made his "complete neutrality" explicit at the outset, but added that he welcomed any European effort to shorten the civil war and to avoid international complications. Delbos, in lieu of British approval of aid to republican Spain, proposed the formula of general non-intervention. Here was a "European effort" similar to

American neutrality. Would non-intervention succeed if the United States formally adhered? Delbos considered this question with the aid of Laboulaye and Jules Henry. No one knew how the revised Neutrality Act would affect American behavior. Henry doubted that Roosevelt would repeat his appeal to legality and reason, which had twice recently failed. Nor would the United States join a collective agreement, because "the fixing of a signature at the bottom of such a declaration would be interpreted as an involvement in European problems." When Roosevelt only informally approved the "non-intervention" formula, Laboulaye inferred that he simply had no plan of his own. His indecision, and the impending presidential election, meant that France would see no important initiative from the White House.

After Roosevelt's re-election in November 1936, Delbos offered another "European initiative": would the President join with France and Britain in a "Gentleman's Agreement" to demand that Generalissimo Franco end the civil war and the tragi-comedy of "non-intervention" through mediation. Warning that "Europe is on the verge of general war," Delbos declared that Anglo-French pressure alone would fail. All depended upon Roosevelt's "unique prestige" in the "moral sphere." Again, the Paris embassy had to reply that Roosevelt, for the time at least, could not "involve himself in rearranging the affairs of the continent of Europe." France must know that the United States would never "under any circumstances guarantee anything in Europe." Still Delbos persisted. Would Roosevelt—or even the American ambassador—simply state publicly that Americans "applauded" the mediation effort in the interests of humanity? Unsuccessfully, Delbos tried again in 1937 and still again in 1938. On the last occasion, Hull replied (with White House approval), "I do not feel that the President would be interested in exploring the idea. . . ."[25]

A Futile Counterpoint, 1936-1937

American reserve did not stifle the mood of mutual friendship and moral accord in Franco-American diplomatic communication. Roosevelt, elusive but sympathetic, elicited French admiration and hope even while refusing to offer the French an alternative to British appeasement. Repeatedly,

French overtures were turned aside, with warm regrets, in a way that the French could not bring themselves to believe was truly final. It seemed that Roosevelt really wished to help, but not at the present moment. The time was never quite right because of domestic pressures, forthcoming elections, or involvement in hemispheric affairs. Or, the President awaited some "European initiative" to which he could effectively react. Yet somehow no French initiative, like Delbos' Spanish mediation proposal, could penetrate the monolithic surface of American neutrality. Two friendly nations carried on a kind of aimless counterpoint, without any foreseeable conclusion.

Intermittently, the French played upon the war debts theme, trying to exchange a debts compromise for some practical form of American "moral support." Léon Blum, during the latter half of 1936, explored this possibility without results. Paris learned that Roosevelt, without rejecting the idea, found it inadvisable to undertake negotiations at that particular time. There would be too much publicity; one should wait until the Congress adjourned; the President might acquire more flexibility from new neutrality legislation early in 1937. In December, William C. Bullitt, now Ambassador in Paris, had to warn Blum against "stirring up bad blood by starting polemics on both sides of the Atlantic on...the debt." No amount of wooing on the debt, Bullitt added, would lead to significant American involvement in Europe. No other tactic "could by hook or by crook" draw Americans into a European war.[26]

Bullitt's appointment as ambassador in mid-1936 itself renewed French hopes, despite the messages he sometimes had to deliver. Perhaps no envoy since Franklin was more popular in France or knew the French people and culture better. According to Georges Bonnet, "he loved our country and considered it almost a second homeland."[27] Bullitt's role had its ironic aspects. He informed the French many times over not to mislead themselves by expecting tangible American aid. And yet his francophilism and the aura of his personal friendship with Roosevelt made it more difficult to convince his French auditors. In late 1936 he privately told Roosevelt that he felt like "the lady who tried to sweep back the sea with a broom. The French want so much to believe that we shall do again what we did in 1917, that one is brushing back constantly a sea of hopes and wishes."[28]

Bullitt's reports to Washington were consistent with his admonitions in Paris. Wary of all attempts to ensnare his country, the Ambassador warned Roosevelt that not only the French, but other European democratic governments had "a violent nervous desire to get us into the next war." Hence, he advised, "we shall have to watch every agreement or other commitment with extreme care if we are to avoid slipping into a position from which there will be no retreat."[29] Yet, for all his lack of guile in influencing the French appraisal of American policy, Bullitt's genuine good will did help the French to lead themselves on, perhaps because they so badly wanted to be led. So the Franco-American counterpoint continued into 1937.

Inadvertently, Bullitt encouraged the French to parlay their waning faith in Roosevelt into one last vision of a tripartite entente to stabilize European peace through massive economic and financial collaboration. When Léon Blum suggested that direct Franco-German negotiations, with American approval, might reduce political tensions and lead to economic cooperation, Bullitt replied that such a *démarche* "would have the full benediction" of his government. To Hull, he recommended informal approval, for he saw a "faint possibility" of success. Spurred by an apparently favorable American attitude, Blum, Delbos, and their financial expert, Emmanuel Monick, inflated Blum's modest proposal into a comprehensive scheme for Franco-British-American economic aid to Europe. In talks with Monick on December 15 and 18, 1936, Bullitt both nourished and evaded French expectations in by now familiar terms. Roosevelt would indeed act for peace, but he had always hesitated because no European nation could devise a detailed plan of action. Were he to receive one, "the vigor with which he would put it to work would perhaps astonish the world." But first, France and Germany must evolve a plan that Roosevelt could support.[30]

From hindsight, Monick's subsequent advice to his government now appears astonishingly ingenuous. France, he urged, had no alternative "to forcing in some fashion. . .an

Anglo-French-American initiative, *whatever it might be* [Monick's italics]." Let France fulfill Roosevelt's condition by talking to Germany and then, regardless of the outcome, present the Americans an outline of what they could consider an "American Plan" for a tripartite European recovery program. If Germany participated, she might return to peaceful ways; if not, she would be isolated, as the program's magnetic attraction drew Italy and others into collaboration. A visionary's dream? As Monick told Bullitt, Britain and France together were "neither rich nor strong enough to buy the peace but anything becomes possible if the three great democracies learn to unite."

Before speaking with Monick, Bullitt had emphasized to Blum and Bonnet that there was not the "slightest chance" of the United States joining any triangular scheme. After hearing Monick, he alerted Roosevelt of a French intent to "involve us in the whole European tangle up to the hilt," including "the next war." In case of a productive Franco-German negotiation, Bullitt advised the President to go no farther than "a general declaration" after prior consultation with Britain and France.[31]

After the Monick plan collapsed, the French did not allow themselves again to imagine a working triangular entente. Until June 1937, Ambassador Georges Bonnet fruitlessly wooed Roosevelt and other prominent Americans in Washington. The futile counterpoint went its usual way. Both Hull and Roosevelt agreed in the abstract with Bonnet's thesis that the "sole way to maintain peace in Europe was a tight union" of the three. But neither man accepted Bonnet's offer to consider any American suggestion for implementing their consensus. From both, Bonnet heard assurances that Roosevelt wished to act in some way, but "does not want to risk a setback." When Roosevelt complained of Britain's "negative attitude," Bonnet reported to Paris that if France could "present him some proposals in concert with the British..., we would have a chance to obtain...a firm and public initiative."

By late spring of 1937, Paris had nothing to offer. Bullitt discerned a spreading defeatism among Delbos and other national leaders. Delbos despaired of "inventing" another peace policy for either the British or Americans to examine, and was "at his wit's end to devise a method" of avoiding utter disaster. The French could suggest only some undefined Rooseveltian intervention, knowing that it would be useless unless the President armed his words "by pledging the support of the armed forces and the economic and financial strength" of his country. That, they agreed, was "impossible." There seemed to be no way out.[32]

With similar convictions, Bonnet left Washington in June. Quite apart from "impossible" pledges, Roosevelt could never issue the sort of blunt international warning that might, as a last resort, deter Hitler. France could only follow the will-o'-the-wisp of America's "intellectual support and moral aid." Even if unforeseen circumstances brought a dramatic reversal in American policy, Bonnet had it from Roosevelt that the United States could not rearm before 1940. He sailed for France with "an unforgettable memory" of his six months in Washington, "the best months of my life."[33] But Bonnet's revised perception of American policy hastened his later recourse to appeasement of Germany.

Apathy in Paris lasted out the year. In mid-July, Hull issued a highly generalized circular statement of American "principles" in international affairs, which he hoped would win a wide consensus abroad. Its neo-Wilsonian flavor was, however, dulled by the reminder: "we avoid entering into alliances or entangling commitments." Hull seemed surprised that France did not respond with a "text," but Delbos attempted no more than ritual praise of good American intentions.[34] Nor did Roosevelt's ephemeral "quarantine the aggressors" speech at Chicago in October arouse more than forlorn approval. Premier Chautemps did not regard it "as promising some action" beyond a vague "moral assistance." But he did tell the American charge, in the latter's words, "that he would give a great deal to be able to sit down quietly with President Roosevelt and ask exactly what he. . .had in mind when he spoke of. . .a concerted effort in opposition to violations of the treaties."[35] As 1937 ended, the French saw few straws worth reaching for.

EPILOGUE: FROM MUNICH TO WAR, 1938-1939

When 1938 began, the French had completed their interwar evaluation of American policy as it related to their security dilemma. Until war came in 1939 there remained nothing more to learn about Roosevelt's response to isolationism. The Franco-British-American triangle would not close. What the French retained of their earlier faith in Roosevelt and American intervention now was merely faith in the original realism of what might have been since 1919. Had Americans been able to equate their own interests with acting as the link between France and Britain, the world of 1938-1939 could have been so different! As Chautemps told Bullitt, if only Roosevelt would declare unequivocally that the United States would oppose aggressors by moral and material aid to peaceful nations, the risk of war would pass, and with it the possibility of America's own later involvement. But this, Chautemps knew, Roosevelt would find politically "impossible."[36]

Therefore, the last French attempts to achieve the impossible during the climactic year 1938 form only an epilogue to this study's primary concern. During the long Czech crisis separating the Nazi absorption of Austria in March and the Munich Pact in September, Franco-American relations produced nothing to impede Hitler's display of unopposed power. Georges Bonnet, as Daladier's foreign minister, time and again appealed for aid in any form, less in the belief that it would really come than as a cry for a miracle to rescue men whose capacity for self-help was exhausted. Would Roosevelt arbitrate the Czech-German dispute? Could the Berlin embassy merely voice its "opinion" that resort to force would be "contrary to the interests of humanity"? Would Hull give even "a discreet affirmation of diplomatic solidarity"? After each overture, Bonnet confronted "an opinion violently hostile to any intervention in Europe." In July, summarizing the opinion of President Lebrun, French generals, and nearly all of the ministers, Bullitt found everyone reduced to hope for American aid in a future war, not to prevent it. Meanwhile Bonnet heard from Bullitt that "definitively, we could expect nothing," including airplanes ordered in May, if war occurred.[37]

War seemed near in late September. Roosevelt called for continued negotiations in a conference of interested parties. Pressed by Bullitt to "let the French out of their moral commitment" to Czechoslovakia, and by Hull to remain aloof,[38] Roosevelt appended to his appeal a clear denial of any intent to become actively involved. To avoid war, his limited intervention could at best further the sort of capitulation which the French and British forthwith made at Munich. For Bonnet, at least, this was "the determining cause" of his nation's plight thereafter.[39]

Between Munich and Hitler's attack on Poland in September 1939, the French looked to America not as the key to peace but as a future source of moral and material assistance in war. And soon after war began, Paul Reynaud spoke in English by radio to the American people and president. At least, he predicted, in a future reconstruction of Europe in some *future* peace, "the role of your country will be a great one."[40]

NOTES

[1] *Entre deux guerres, souvenirs sur la IIIe République*, II (Paris: Plon, 1945), 9. Hereafter, unless otherwise cited, quoted material is drawn from published French documents, upon which the bulk of my analysis for the 1930's is based: Ministère des Affaires Etrangères, *Documents diplomatiques français, 1932-1939* (Paris: Imprimerie Nationale, 1963-1972), Series 1 (1932-1935), Vols. I-VI (July 19, 1932-July 26, 1934), and Series 2 (1936-1939), Vols. I-V (Jan. 1, 1936-May 31, 1937).

[2] For France's response to the peace, particularly its effect upon Franco-British relations, see Arnold Wolfers, *Britain and France Between Two Wars* (New York: Harcourt, Brace, 1940).

[3] Pierre-Etienne Flandin, *Politique française, 1919-1940* (Paris: Editions Nouvelles, 1947), p. 88.

[4] *Jadis*, II (Paris: Flammarion, 1952), 647.

[5] Pierre Renouvin, *Histoire des relations internationales*, VIII (Paris: Librairie Hachette, 1957), 357.

[6] Herriot, II, 128.

[7] Jean Baptiste Duroselle, *From Wilson to Roosevelt: Foreign Policy of the United States, 1913-1945*, trans. by Nancy Lyman Roelker (Cambridge, Mass.: Harvard University Press, 1963), p. 448.

[8] Flandin, p. 80.

[9] *Ibid*, pp. 77-78.

[10] André Tardieu, *L'Heure de la décision* (Paris: E. Flammarion, 1934), quotations in order, pp. 12, 14.

[11] Henry L. Stimson and McGeorge Bundy, *On Active Service in Peace and War* (New York: Harper & Brothers, 1947), p. 277.

[12] *Mémoires* (Paris: E. Flammarion, 1963), I, 350.

[13] Paul-Boncour, II, 222. Also see Georges Bonnet, *De Washington au Quai d'Orsay* (Genève: Constant Bourquin, 1946), pp. 113-14. Hereafter cited as *Quai d'Orsay*.

[14] France. Assemblee Nationale, *Les événements survenus en France de 1933 à 1945 (témoignages et documents recueillis par la commission d'enquête parlementaire)*, Vol. III (Paris: Presses Universitaires de France, n.d.), No. 2344, *séance* of Feb. 3, 1948, p. 607.

[15] Tardieu, pp. 27-38.

[16] Paul-Boncour, II, 272, 375-76.

[17] Claudel letter to Herriot, Feb. 17, 1933, as quoted by Herriot, II, 361-62.

[18] This interpretation is solidly supported by John David Hauser, "Britain, France, and the United States at the World Economic Conference of 1933: A Study in Futility," (unpublished Ph.D.

43

dissertation, Washington State University, 1973); pp. 152-215.

[19]Private letter to Reynaud, Jan. 9, 1934, as quoted by Reynaud, I, 411.

[20]Herriot, II, 424-26, 433 (quoted passage, p. 426).

[21]Orville H. Bullitt, ed., *For the President Personal and Secret. Correspondence between Franklin D. Roosevelt and William C. Bullitt* (Boston: Houghton Mifflin Co., 1972), Nov. 8, 1936, p. 179. Hereafter cited as *For the President*.

[22]Reynaud, II, 88.

[23]Brice Harris, Jr., *The United States and the Italo-Ethiopian Crisis* (Stanford: Stanford University Press, 1964), pp. 103-19.

[24]United States Department of State, *Foreign Relations of the United States* 1936, I: Straus to Hull, March 8, 1936, p. 217; Hull to Straus, March 10, 1936, p. 228; Hull to Roosevelt, March 9, p. 218. Hereafter cited as *FRUS*.

[25]*FRUS*, 1936, II, Bullitt to Hull, Nov. 28 and Dec. 10, pp. 578-81, 607; 1938, I, Bullitt to Hull, Jan. 25, pp. 152-53, and Hull to Bullitt, Jan. 26, p. 153.

[26]*FRUS*, 1936, I: Straus to Hull, May 14 and 19, pp. 582, 584; Bullitt to Hull, Dec. 1 and 10, pp. 586-90.

[27]Bonnet, *Quai d'Orsay*, p. 206.

[28]Bullitt, *For the President*, Dec. 8, 1936, p. 198.

[29]*Ibid.*, Nov. 24, 1936, pp. 184-85.

[30]*FRUS*, 1936, I: Bullitt to Hull.

[31]Bullitt, *For the President*, Dec. 7, 20, pp. 194-96, 200-02.

[32]*FRUS*, 1937, I: Bullitt to Hull, May 6, 1937, pp. 89-92.

[33]*Défense de la paix* (Genève, Editions du Cheval Aile, 1946-1948), II, 26-27, 174.

[34]*FRUS*, 1937, I: "Statement by the Secretary of State," July 16, pp. 699-700; Hull (personal) to Bullitt, Aug. 2, p. 741; Bullitt to Hull, Aug. 4, pp. 749-50.

[35]*FRUS*, 1937, I: Wilson to Hull, Oct. 6, pp. 135-36.

[36]*FRUS*, 1938, I: Bullitt to Hull, Jan. 4, 1938, p. 2.

[37]Bonnet, *Quai d'Orsay*, pp. 2-13. *FRUS*; 1938, I: Bullitt to Hull, May 22 (pp. 512-15), July 13 (pp. 529-32), Sept. 12 (p. 589).

[38]FRUS, 1938, I: "personal for the president," May 22, p. 510; Bullitt, *For the President*, p. 296.

[39]Bonnet, *Quai d'Orsay*, p. 232.

[40]Reynaud, II, 293.

PERSPECTIVE

Though the three European powers variously appraised one another's alliance potential in the 1930s, they separately arrived at a common perception of American foreign policy. In Professor Callahan's terms, the British knew that Americans offered "only words" to the cause of European security. These were words which, as Professor Bennett concludes for the Russians, amounted to "no policy but merely an attitude." In their turn the French made a parallel discovery and, like the others, found no way to translate American diplomatic ambiguity into action for collective security. If, as Bennett observes, it was galling in Moscow to realize that the Americans failed to equate present threats to European and Far Eastern peace with their own ultimate security, this was equally so in Paris and London.

But consensus on the intrinsic limitations in American policy did not foster a cooperative adjustment to it. Rather, and fatefully for European peace, the three powers veered apart through a balance-of-power hiatus widened by American isolationism. Each of the three, in its own time, accepted the American refusal to join any security system. Whereupon each sought refuge in divergent policies which sacrificed the national interests of all. Britain, unable to reassemble the elements of a traditional balance of power, charted a course of onesided "appeasement." Despairing of any real "organization of the peace," France capitulated to her dependence upon Britain. And the Soviet Union, failing to escape its former isolation by a "common front against fascism" with the West, turned instead to a transient pact with Hitler in 1939. This divergence during the critical 1930s sprang from earlier differences of objectives and attitudes unrelated to American policy. But the international results of differences among the three also reflected their respective historical experiences in dealing with a common "American problem."

Since about 1900 the British had nurtured their "special relationship" with the United States. They had found it expedient to withdraw the Royal Navy's presence from the

Western Hemisphere and elsewhere tactfully to avoid collisions with the Americans because they understood the younger nation's isolationist posture, not because they hoped to change it. Pressed by Germany and others in the pre-1914 European balance and in imperialist confrontations around the globe, Britain realistically adapted to the Americans' unilateral "diplomacy" and their tendency to equate self-interest with higher moral values. Britain's far-sighted intent was to appease another potential rival, not to groom a future ally. Hence the ensuing "special relationship," so well described by Callahan, lived upon the prewar British insight that even though the United States refused to play the diplomatic game by European rules and would probably never commit herself specifically to Britain, neither would she consort with Britain's adversaries. In such a tenuous and imperfect trans-Atlantic relationship it was better unilaterally to adjust than to confront, prudently to cater than to ask or expect tangible favors. But the subtleties of this British policy demanded restraint in contracting with other powers any obligations which might lead Britain into conflict with American interests. Anything else would jeopardize the intangible value in what Callahan considers a semi-mythical Anglo-American friendship. Not presuming to view America as a possible ally, the British must more carefully look to their own resources and count their limitations.

In the postwar years the British could easily verify the lessons of their earlier experience with the "special relationship." Thus when Callahan tells us that during the 1920s the United States dealt her former "associated power" (not ally) a "series of savage blows" in matters of seapower, imperial security—especially in the Far East—and war debts, this is to say that the British had older perceptions reconfirmed. Callahan also refers to an American "ambivalence" that baffled the British; but one might go farther to conclude that they understood it only too well. For, again following Callahan, when in the early 1930s the "special relationship" was strained anew by the debts, the Johnson Act, Imperial Preference, and security issues in the Far East, London saw no reason thereafter to count upon future American security pledges. Now the prewar lesson was

46

twice reconfirmed.

Drawn also by Commonwealth influences into concerns beyond Europe, the British had to reappraise their own resources both on the Continent and in the Far East. Unwilling to reckon France a reliable co-deterrent against Germany, and viewing Soviet collaboration as both risky and repugnant, Britain sought to husband her total resources by the policy of appeasement in Europe, the better to deploy those resources in support of her world position. Despite an only partly-realized intention to rearm, that decision boded ill for a containment of Germany if appeasement failed. It made even "moral" alignment with the United States, in the absence of reciprocal commitments, a possible liability in dealing with Germany—and hence, a further rationale for appeasement. Thereby it also negated French hopes for a "triangular" entente including either the United States or the Soviet Union.

Postwar France, more than Britain, misread the concept of a "special relationship," and doubly so. Ironically, considering Britain's longer experience with the "American problem," the French tended to infer far more collusion between the "Anglo-Saxons" than really existed. It followed that if France could cultivate her own "special relationship" with the United States, she could rebuild the bridge to Britain and restore the triangular security arrangement lost in 1919. Before 1914, unlike the British, the French had not been driven by their world interests seriously to woo the Americans and to take a hard look at both the possibilities and limits of closer Franco-American relations. Perceiving no need to probe American isolation further, they could abide with a vague "friendship" image. Their realistic appraisal of the United States as an element of French security in Europe began only at war's end, out of necessity. American isolationism had to be re-examined suddenly, amidst immediate anxiety for the future of France.

Thus the French readjustment proceeded with more real ambivalence than was apparent in Britain's experience. Paris was unable to accept as stoically the "no policy" image of American isolation. In Franco-American relations flurries of resentment openly alternated with hopes of drawing the

United States into participation in a European security scheme wherein Far Eastern concerns were quite secondary. Hopes persisted because fewer security alternatives were visible in Paris than in London. Like Britain, France knew the frustrated irritation of wondering why the Americans could not see where their own longer-range interests lay. Meanwhile, pending some American *démarche* toward Europe, enough French irritation was left over to include the British, also apparently blind to their common interests with France on the Continent. So, ruefully assessing American isolationism for what it was, but driven by the pressures of 1930s, the French could still pray that a Stimson or a Roosevelt would lead Americans out of their "no policy" wilderness and thereby educate the British as well. Not until 1937 did they arrive at the perception of American policy with which the British began the crisis of the thirties. By then, French alternatives were reduced to a reluctant dependence upon British appeasement. The Franco-Soviet Alliance of 1935, conceived in ambiguity, was only a wraith, awaiting the unlikely moment when British acquiescence might give it new life.

Though Soviet leaders were the last to explore the prospects of alignment with the United States, they ended with conclusions similar to those of the British and the French. If they nourished their hopes a little longer, it was not in full confidence. Professor Bennett's portrayal of Molotov straining in Moscow to "fathom" the "cloudy" surface of American isolationism would have evoked old memories, though not nostalgia, across the Channel. Litvinov's plaint, "we are always expecting more than we should from America," had its earlier counterpart in Paris. To arrive at even these ambiguous expectations in the 1930s had required a revision of the initial Bolshevik view of America after 1917.

Having rejected the legacy of their Tsarist predecessors (who might have transmitted some useful insights into American policy), the Communists during the early 1920s had no reason to revise at close hand their stereotype of "capitalist" America playing the armed "imperialist" in the Allied Intervention of 1918-19. There was no hope of diplomatic partnership with such a power, much less an impulse to seek it. But, as Bennett indicates without using the term, subsequent international experiences in an unfriendly world superimposed a certain "communist realism" over the ideological matrix of Soviet attitudes toward foreign relations. Opportunistic diplomacy on behalf of immediate national interests, pursued through a rebuilt diplomatic apparatus, complemented a long-range revolutionary internationalism centered in the Party and the Comintern. Each agency furthered the policy needs of the other. Ideologically, the Soviet Union became the "base" of distant global revolution; pragmatically, the furtherance of Soviet national goals by all available means fused with the pursuit of ideological objectives.

If such a flexible ambivalence served Soviet security concerns in the twenties, it could also serve amidst the international crises of the thirties. Why, then, not ascribe a parallel sort of empiricism to the Americans? As dogmatic capitalists and isolationists by preference the Yankees must be regarded with distrust and diplomatic prudence. But as self-seeking "imperialists" they were potential, if temporary, collaborators should Soviet and American world interests be imperilled by a common foe. When the latter contingency arose, it was only "communist realism" to probe for a corresponding American "isolationist realism" adaptable to the defense of converging interests.

In 1933 the Recognition Agreement was such a probe. Therefore it became a source of subsequent diplomacy whose results we may compare with the two western powers' respective encounters with American policy. Analogous to French anti-German strategy in Europe was the Soviet vision of a "triangular" containment of Japan in the Far East. Indirectly, at least, a Russo-American (and British) entente might evolve from collaboration with the League. As a step toward that end after Recognition, Soviet policy manipulated the Russo-American debts issue as a quid pro quo for a bilateral non-aggression pact. This tactic was no more successful than the concurrent French refusal of war debt payments as a fulcrum for pressing the Americans into a consultative pact or another form of "moral" commitment in Europe. In neither case did American elusiveness squelch the sporadic flareups of optimism in Moscow and Paris until 1937 and 1938, respectively. Both France and the U.S.S.R., having gauged the depths of isolationism in the American people and Congress, nonetheless awaited some timely Rooseveltian intervention in support of mutual security. To borrow and extend Bennett's judgment of Soviet hopes, we can say that both wishfully "continued to grasp at every apparent gesture" from the White House. When Roosevelt's Quarantine Speech of 1937 and its negative aftermath fell short of the long-anticipated *tour de force*, the French and Russians were alone with American ambiguity.

Britain, also in need of American support in the Far East and Europe, scarcely expected it in either area. Her sense of self-interest in relation to American Far Eastern policy, from the Washington Treaties through the Hoover-Stimson Doctrine of 1932, dimmed the prospect of even a bilateral, much less "triangular," front against Japan. Callahan refers to a "marked distrust" of American motives well before the Quarantine Speech. The British, despite a transitory "Gentlemen's Agreement" with the French at Lausanne in 1932, were more conciliatory on the war debt issue, more from concern with preserving whatever remained of the "special relationship" than with making it more tangible. Meanwhile they had already embarked upon their complementary Far Eastern and European policies, neither of which contemplated alignment with the U.S.S.R. or the United States. Even the presence of a William C. Bullitt—at once a catalyst of reawakened hope and a damper upon specific expectations in Moscow and Paris—would not have changed the British position. American ambiguity, as Callahan writes, "helped to set the limits beyond which successive British governments felt it impossible to go."

If so, neither French nor Russian diplomacy could achieve its goals in Europe. The French were uninterested in any Far Eastern arrangement except as a step toward collaboration in Europe. When both in the Far East and at the Disarmament and World Economic Conferences during 1932-1934 the Americans continued in their isolated ways, it became clear that appeasement was the British alternative to a western "triangle" in Europe. At that juncture France ran out of policy options, including her wooing of the U.S.S.R. during

50

1934-35 in the League, in an "Eastern Locarno" scheme, and in the Franco-Soviet Pact that the French nearly stifled with escape clauses during its birth. Without British participation or approval, France's eastward reorientation was bound to become abortive. Similarly, the Soviet approach to France could not be productive unless Britain were included in the system, as the Munich Pact demonstrated in 1938 and the fruitless Soviet-British alliance negotiations reconfirmed between April and July, 1939. Thereafter the Soviets turned abruptly eastward into the Nazi-Soviet Pact of August. The sequels of that realignment included the German attack on Poland, the dissolution of Anglo-French appeasement in another war, Germany's sudden destruction of Soviet neutrality in June, 1941—and the ultimate "entanglement" of the United States following Pearl Harbor.

Can we therefore accept Callahan's apparent selection of American isolationist policy as an indirect yet decisive cause in such a disastrous chain-reaction of events? I agree that Britain—and we may add France and the U.S.S.R.—had to share the costs which even Americans eventually paid for their negative interwar role. But could the European powers, even in face of an American default, have themselves joined to salvage the debris of European security? In fact, did their perceptions of American policy become self-serving rationalizations for inaction based upon other reasons? Perhaps these questions are unanswerable; but they are implicit in all three of the studies in this volume.

Callahan speculates that even American support of the League in 1935 and afterward would not have diluted Baldwin's and Chamberlain's pessimism regarding the chances of containing Nazi Germany. From Bennett's analysis, though he is less clear on the point, one might infer that the Russians were already ambivalent because of their inherent suspicions of the West and the policy dilemma stemming from their position between Europe and the Far East. They may have found a perverse comfort in blaming their inaction (until 1939), and then their *démarche* toward Germany, upon American myopia and even an imagined "conspiracy" with the appeasers, as an attempt to deflect Germany eastward against the Soviet Union. Yet, alone among the four powers before Munich, the Soviet Union outwardly seemed willing to mobilize League resources and her French and Czechoslovak agreements, if assured of Anglo-French reciprocity. As much could be said for the Soviet role in the alliance negotiations of April-July, 1939—provided now that the two western powers were willing to pay the price of a Soviet commitment in a new post-appeasement situation. Diplomatic ambiguity was neither exclusively Anglo-French nor American! The French, even in the twenties haunted by their sense of dependence upon Britain in Europe so long as America held aloof, could logically use that implicit premise to cover their fear of taking any independent initiative. If the United States were the only discernible bridge to a viable anti-German bloc, then American inaction ever since the abortive triangular pact of 1919 explained the defeat of French security aspirations in the 1930s.

These three studies focus upon European "perceptions." But we cannot ignore that the latter were influenced by American perceptions, accurate or not, of the European powers. Callahan pointedly locates the essence of Anglo-American relations from 1919 to 1941 in the truism that no power commits itself to another "except for value received." Perhaps the Europeans—or at least the French and Russians—overvalued a desirable American intervention which they had no sound reason to expect. Conversely, the Americans saw too little value in fulfilling European expectations which they considered unwarranted. As William C. Bullitt's private correspondence with Roosevelt forcefully reminds us, a popular American isolationist stereotype was also shared in high places: Europeans, rather than joining for their common security, were separately conniving to lure the United States into conflicts irrelevant to truly American interests.

Roosevelt's repeated requests for some "European initiative" to which he might react may have been a way to evade uttering a more positive policy which he could neither clearly conceive nor risk taking without support at home. Yet, given the limits upon his own initiative and Britain's intention to appease Germany and shun the U.S.S.R., what "value" could he perceive in extending more definite verbal assurances? For similar and also different reasons, including the ideological chasm that still yawned after Recognition, what value could Roosevelt assign to closer association with the U.S.S.R. until the latter suddenly bore the full impact of Nazi power in the drastically new conditions of 1941? As for France, whose "ingratitude" was sharply etched upon the American image of interwar Europe, her value only appeared at the moment of its disappearance in the disaster of June, 1940 and in the consequent peril of Britain, left alone in war.

Perhaps the French had been overly obsessed with their triangular dilemma. But what they had long dreaded, were the Americans not to identify their own interests with Europe, had now come all too literally true. In a clash of "misperceptions," the four powers had managed to cancel out one another's best intentions.

EXPECT ONLY WORDS:

ANGLO-AMERICAN RELATIONS 1919-41[1]

by

Raymond Callahan

The Second World War lies like a great scar across the face of the twentieth century. After the 1914-18 war there was an attempt to put the pre-war order of things back together again. No one even tried after 1945. The seminal nature of the war imparts to inquiries into its origins much of their fascination and importance. Could it have been avoided? When was the point of no return passed—1931? 1933? 1936? 1938? Who was responsible? Hitler, certainly. But what of the leaders of the democracies? Could their errors have contributed as much to the final tragedy as the policy of Hitler? Winston Churchill and the historian A.J.P. Taylor have argued, from their very different perspectives, that British leadership—timid, blinkered, and unimaginative—bears much of the blame for the catastrophe. Neither said much about the role American policy played in shaping that of Britain. Churchill was always very careful in what he wrote about the United States from motives of sentiment and policy; otherwise, he might well have quoted Neville Chamberlain's irritated (but not unjust) remark: "It is always best and safest to count on nothing from the Americans but words."[1a] Taylor dismissed America's role with the observation that it was a power that sought only to be left alone. But even for being left alone there is a price. In this case the price was paid largely by others.

British policy in the face of Hitler was determined by a number of factors, many of them domestic and largely beyond the influence of any foreign power, hostile or friendly. But American attitudes helped to set the limits beyond which successive British governments felt it impossible to go. British views of what America would, or would not do, played their part in the coming of the Second World War.

I

To put the events of the nineteen thirties in perspective, it is necessary to review briefly the principal characteristics and salient events of Anglo-American relations following America's emergence as a world power at the end of the nineteenth century. At that time, after a century during which relations

57

ranging from indifferent to acerbic, the British government made a fundamental change in its attitude towards the United States. The British became conscious of being badly over-extended, of being a "weary titan" in Joseph Chamberlain's trenchant phrase. From the Boer War (1899-1902) on, British policy sought to reduce Britain's isolation and vulnerability in order to address itself more effectively to the principal challenge: Imperial Germany. Part of this process consisted of improving relations with the United States. This had gone far enough by 1908 for the British government to decide that a war with America was "so unlikely as to be a contingency against which it is unnecessary to make provision."[2] In the following year the Two-Power Standard—the doctrine that the Royal Navy must be able to meet the next two largest fleets in combination—was abandoned in favor of a sixty per cent superiority in dreadnoughts over Germany alone. The cost of the naval race with Germany, plus the cost of newly introduced social welfare legislation, left the British with no other choice. They could no longer match the world. It is important, however, to be clear about the implications of these little-noticed events. Britain did not have (and would not get until the signing of the North Atlantic Treaty in 1949) a formal treaty with America. There was therefore no *quid pro quo* for taking American off the "potential enemies" list. Rather, there was incurred an additional obligation—the burden imposed on British diplomacy of seeing that relations with the United States did in fact remain friendly. Disputes with America would in the long run be settled on the best terms that could be gotten out of the Americans, since no other course of action was possible. Appeasement had begun.

Britain's need to keep on the best possible terms with a power that, for various reasons, could not be tied up in the normal fashion made it important to establish that Anglo-American relations existed on a different, and higher, plane. This was the origin of the convenient and long-lived myth that was eventually to be christened "the special relationship." There was of course some validity to it. Ties of language, literature, law, institutions and shared history do bind England and the United States in a unique way. Anglo-American relations did certainly grow warmer during

58

the Edwardian years. Some of this was due to the simple fact that the English were making concessions, some to the social ties forged between England and the United States, although this factor, because it is easy and interesting to chronicle, has certainly been overvalued. Much more was owing to the climate of the times: America's brief fling at overt imperialism, Britain's sympathy with the United States during the Spanish-American War, and the prevailing Social Darwinism of an age which produced the concept of "Anglo-Saxondom." The British, to whom the idea of a "special relationship" had become very important, did a better job of convincing themselves of its validity than of converting the Americans. In the beginning, as at the end, they were its greatest devotees because they needed it more.

It is doubtful if many Englishmen ever really grasped the deep-seated ambivalence with which most Americans viewed Britain. True, there were the links beloved of the English-Speaking Union, and large numbers of Anglophiles. But there was also the national myth enshrined in every elementary school history primer: the United States originated in a revolt against the tyranny of the British Empire. Dwight Eisenhower, who knew a great deal about the subject, was to write to George Marshall in 1943 that most Anglo-American misunder-standings had their roots in those primers.[3] Added to this was the presence of large numbers of Americans of non "Anglo-Saxon" stock who were indifferent or hostile to America's English heritage. There was also a thrust by American politicians and businessmen for a "place in the sun" commensurate with America's power and wealth. These were ingredients for a "special relationship" of a rather different sort, and on the American side it is probably the only "special relationship" that ever existed. The inexorable pressure of strategic and economic facts dictated the policy the British government followed. If they erred, it was in placing too much credence in the value of the stage properties with which they surrounded it.

II

The real nature of Anglo-American relations is clearly

displayed during the First World War and its immediate aftermath. Once war began, Britain was increasingly dependent upon her continuing ability to buy American supplies and then to borrow American money. American doctrines of neutral rights posed as great an immediate threat to the maritime supremacy upon which Britain depended as the 1916 and 1918 naval construction programs and Wilson's "Freedom of the Seas" did to its future. Had it not been for German policy, Anglo-American relations would have been much worse. Even when the United States entered the war in 1917 it was as an "associate," not as an ally. It was only after the Armistice, however, that the full consequences of the emergence of America became apparent. In the four years following the German collapse, the United States dealt Britain a series of savage blows, forcing her to surrender formally her maritime supremacy and at the same time to abandon the only security she had, in the absence of dominance at sea, for her huge eastern empire. It was the British Empire's greatest defeat since the loss of the American colonies.

There is tremendous irony in what happened in 1918-22. Few could have imagined on November 11, 1918 that within four years a British government would quitely surrender, at the behest of another power, both the Royal Navy's traditional superiority and a strategically crucial alliance, for never had Great Britain and her Empire looked so imposing. Appearances were deceiving, however. The war had shaken Britain to the core, and the full effects were apparent only in retrospect. Britain's economy, already ailing before 1914, had sustained major damage. Financial pre-eminence was lost to New York. The self-confidence that was England's secret weapon during the nineteenth century was dealt a blow from which it never quite recovered. In short, it was a shaken and a poorer country that faced the problems of the postwar world. It was, moreover, a country in the process of an almost silent, largely bloodless, social revolution. As embodied in the Labour Party, which after 1918 rapidly replaced the failing Liberals as the alternative to the Conservatives, it cared far more about housing, schools, and jobs than about battleships and the outposts of Empire. Finally the Empire, itself seemingly such a solid prop of British power in 1918, was beginning to disintegrate. The nationalism that wrenched Southern Ireland away and led to major advances towards self-government in India was obvious. Less so was the growing nationalism of the "old dominions"—Canada, Australia, New Zealand, and South Africa—which was turning them into allies to be conciliated rather than subordinates whose support could be assumed. As yet all this amounted only to cracks in a still imposing facade—but those cracks indicated that the foundations had begun to shift. British policymakers were at least dimly aware of what was happening, and this was the reason why the American pressure on the Royal Navy and the Anglo-Japanese alliance produced little resistance and finally procured complete surrender.

The roots of the American thrust towards a "navy second to none" lay in the navalism of the late nineteenth and early twentieth centuries and, more generally, in the thrust toward world power status produced by America's vaulting strength. The wartime naval building program enbodied the goals of the "big navy" men and their political and industrial backers. A navy second to none meant a navy equal to the Royal Navy. Not suprisingly in a service that measured itself against its British counterpart, Anglophobia was prominent among United States Navy officers, including Admiral William Benson, the Chief of Naval Operations. The tension generated by the incipient rivalry between the two navies surfaced in the spring of 1919 in what has been called "the sea battle of Paris."[4] Benson and his British counterpart, the First Sea Lord, Admiral Sir Rosslyn Wemyss, had a personal clash so intense that one onlooker feared they would come to blows. Some British naval officers were even reported to be talking about a preventative war to scotch America's naval pretensions. The First Lord, Walter Long, told Benson, more tactfully but equally firmly, that "the supremacy of the British Navy was an absolute necessity, not only for the very existence of the British Empire but even of the peace of the world."[5] Brave words, but Lloyd George realized that an open break with the United States on the naval issue was impossible, and a compromise was struck. The British agreed that the Americans could insert a reservation concerning the Monroe Doctrine in the Covenant of the League of Nations, while the Americans agreed to consider postponing the construction of those ships of the 1916 program that had not yet been laid down, and held out the hope that the 1918 program might be cancelled altogether. It was a compromise from which the Americans gained far more than the British. This was to be the pattern of many future Anglo-American agreements.

The issue of whether the British would maintain their maritime supremacy, even at the cost of a naval race and consequent strained relations with America, was still pending, however. In the eighteen months following the "sea battle of Paris" it became apparent that such a competition was out of the question. Britain simply could not afford it—as Lloyd George pointed out, the Americans could win before the race began just by demanding the immediate repayment of Britain's immense wartime indebtedness. In any case, the British public, weary after four years of war, and with the promise of "homes fit for heros" still ringing in their ears, would not have been very likely to accept an immensely expensive arms race with America as an adequate substitute. Far from building up its fighting services, the British government was ruthlessly cutting them down in 1919-20. By the spring of 1920 British naval policy had been redefined. Walter Long, introducing the 1920-21 naval estimates in March, told the House of Commons that it was British policy to maintain a navy "not. . .inferior in strength to the Navy of any other Power."[6] Thus ended a tradition dating back to the eighteenth century, by which the Royal Navy had always been maintained at a strength superior to any other fleet. Long's announcement marks one of the most important phases in the decline and fall of the British Empire.

Even the decision to accept parity with the United States did not settle the matter, because it was necessary to define parity. Furthermore, by the time the British accepted the idea of naval equality with the United States, a new problem had arisen to complicate the issue—the future of the Anglo-Japanese alliance. The British had never intended to allow themselves to be drawn into a clash with America because of the alliance, and the Japanese had been told as much. The alliance, moreover, was no longer regarded as really adequate protection for Britain's Far Eastern interests. Even before the end of the war the Admiralty had been concerned about a potential Japanese threat and had investigated the possibility of building up a fleet, with substantial contingents from India and the dominions, to counter it. But naval equality with the United States, plus the jettisoning of the Anglo-Japanese alliance, posed an insoluble problem. Britain would be giving up whatever residual cover for her interests the alliance still provided. She would also be giving up by treaty the ability to build a fleet of the size necessary to defend those interests herself. Admittedly, the chances of actually being able to build such a fleet were very slight, but, such as they were, they were now to be surrendered. Britain was fixed by geography in Europe; her fleet would equally be fixed in Atlantic and Mediterranean waters by any hostilities or even by high levels of tension there. In that case, what defense would remain for her Far Eastern interests, or for Australia and New Zealand, against Japan? The answer, too painful to be faced squarely, was that there would be none. In the climactic discussion on December 14, 1920, when the Committee of Imperial Defence (the focus of Britain's strategic planning) thrashed out the interlocked issues of future naval policy and the Anglo-Japanese alliance, Winston Churchill stated bluntly that "no more fatal policy" could be imagined for Britain than to seem to be aligning itself with Japan against the United States. Lloyd George snapped back that there was one more fatal course, "namely one whereby we would be at the mercy of the United States."[7] Lloyd George was right. Unless America would enter into a formal alliance that would shield Britain's interests in the Pacific and Far East, the British would be sacrificing their alliance with Japan in the mere hope of American goodwill. And America was not prepared, then or later, to underwrite Britain's position "east of Suez."

Churchill, however, was also right—Britain could not afford to alienate the United States over the Japanese alliance, especially since doing so would also alienate Canada. The Canadians shared some of the American dislike of Japan, but even more they had an obvious stake in good Anglo-American relations. The Anglo-Japanese alliance was doomed by these converging pressures. On June 16, 1921 the cabinet approved the Admiralty's plan to build a great naval base on Singapore Island so that the Royal Navy could, if need arose, be redeployed to the Far East. Despite its obvious weaknesses, this promise to send the main fleet to Singapore (if it was free when the time came) became the basis of British defense policy in the Far East, since there was no other alternative. On the 29th the Canadian Prime Minister, in London for an Imperial Conference, publicly demanded the abrogation of the Anglo-Japanese alliance. Within a fortnight the United States government had called for a conference to be held in Washington on naval and Pacific matters.

The Washington Conference was a milestone in a great many respects. Two matters of vital interest to Britain—her naval policy and the security of her immense eastern interests—were now settled in a foreign capital. It was an event that was to become commonplace in the next fifty years. Her maritime supremacy vanished with the agreement on a 5-5-3 ration for American, British and Japanese capital ship strength respectively. The Japanese alliance was replaced by a number of platitudinous agreements. The Americans had accomplished their aims and had given nothing in return. Indeed, reality was worse than appearance. The Washington Treaty limits on naval strength, and the accompanying prohibition against any British or American fortified bases west of Hawaii or north of Singapore, left Japan dominant in the western Pacific. As security for Australia, New Zealand and other imperial interests in the area, the British had plans for a base at Singapore, and the hope that they would be able to send a fleet there if the need arose. They also entertained the hope that by meeting American wishes they had won American goodwill and thus achieved an understanding with Washington that would do duty for the more formal alliance they could not have. The "special relationship" was to be relied upon again.

Goodwill was not very evident in 1923 when Stanley Baldwin (Chancellor of the Exchequer in the Conservative government that had replaced Lloyd George's coalition in the autumn of 1922) went to Washington to negotiate a settlement of Britain's wartime debts to the United States. The

British had proposed a cancellation all around which, in restrospect, would have been much the wisest thing to do. This found no favor in America, however, and Baldwin had eventually to accept a settlement on very stiff terms, so stiff in fact that he exceeded his instructions in agreeing to them. On his return to London, there was a row of major proportions. At one moment it seemed as if the Prime Minister, Andrew Bonar Law, would resign rather than agree to the terms Baldwin had brought back. In the end the cabinet stayed together and honored Baldwin's signature. The British paid faithfully until the economic crisis of the early thirties put an end to the whole war debts and reparations tangle. Since this settlement was the most onerous inflicted on any wartime "associate," Britain might have been expected to reap some credit for accepting and fulfilling it as long as she could. It is symbolic of the real state of Anglo-American relations that such credit as was handed out for the payment of war debts was garnered by "honest Finland," which paid its miniscule war debt in full.

Many British officials who were engaged in the naval and financial negotiations of 1922-23 developed a jaundiced view of the United States. Two are particularly important: Sir Warren Fisher, the Permanent Under-Secretary to the Treasury and Head of the Civil Service, and Sir Maurice Hankey, Secretary to both the Cabinet and the Committee of Imperial Defence. Even in a country where civil servants normally exercise a great deal of power, these two men were unusual in the influence they were able to wield. Fisher had been involved in the debt settlement negotiations with the United States; Hankey was passionately committed to maintaining British seapower. Neither had the slightest belief in the "special relationship." Since Hankey was a powerful influence with Baldwin (Prime Minister 1923-24, 1925-29, 1935-37) and Fisher with Neville Chamberlain (Prime Minister 1937-40), their views had great significance—a fact to which I will return. Many British naval officers were also Americanophobe after the events of 1919-22. As late as the early thirties one senior officer remarked that it was by no means certain that America would not be on the opposite side in a future war.[8]

This irritability was understandable since the naval rivalry, with its depressing effect on British naval strength, was by no means terminated by the Washington agreements. It sputtered on for the rest of the decade, centering on the question of cruiser strength. The argument was complicated and technical, but essentially the United States Navy wanted a number of large, heavily-gunned cruisers—the great expanse of the Pacific was already gripping American naval thought. The British, with globe-girdling trade routes to protect, wanted a larger number of smaller, more lightly-armed cruisers. One attempt to square this particular circle broke down at Geneva in 1927, sending Anglo-American relations to a new low. The issue was settled three years later, at the 1930 London Naval Conference, but only because the Prime Minister, Ramsay Macdonald, took the matter out of the hands of the Admiralty, who had largely controlled the 1927 discussions, and imposed a settlement on American terms by which the British agreed to the American figure of fifty cruisers for each navy. The Admiralty had insisted that seventy was the absolute minimum needed if the Royal Navy was to discharge the duties that would fall upon it in wartime. The date of the compromise is significant. The Great Depression was deepening, and the British had hopes of renegotiating the whole war debts issue. Hitler had not yet come to power; Japan had not yet begun her move into Manchuria; Italy was not yet hostile. Macdonald's decision was not as fatuous as hindsight makes it appear. Yet the decision, taken in response to American pressure (pressure that did not flow from any real concern for American security but rather from the desire to assert equality, for equality's sake, with Britain) was nearly disastrous. For the Admiralty's contention that it needed at least seventy cruisers turned out to be amply justified. When war came nine years later Britain had too few cruisers. It is of course by no means certain that British governments would have authorized the construction of an adequate number of cruisers even if the treaty had not been signed. What is certain is that in the quest for American goodwill, the British government imposed upon the Royal Navy a formal upper limit to British cruiser strength which the Admiralty knew to be seriously inadequate. If any measure is sought of the importance which successive British governments placed on

American friendship, there is none more striking than this overriding of the hitherto sacrosanct advice of the Royal Navy concerning matters of imperial defense.

At the cost of the Admiralty's discomfiture, the 1930s began with Anglo-American relations apparently on the mend. Like the war debts, the naval issues had been settled on America's terms, and there were no current issues that seemed likely to upset things. The world slump soon took care of that.

III

The consequences of the economic crisis of 1931 for Anglo-American relations were momentous. Britain abandoned both the gold standard and free trade. It introduced protection for the home market, and the Ottawa Conference of 1932 then established a system of tariff rebates within the Empire, known as imperial preference. Even worse, the British "defaulted" on their war debts. The inverted commas are justified since payment was made nearly impossible by the high level of American tariffs, which severely curtailed the sale of goods in the United States, thus blocking the only way the British could earn the dollars necessary to pay. After the expiration of the Hoover moratorium, the British hoped to renegotiate to whole issue. This they were unable to do, and, with the drying up of German reparation payments, they were simply unable to carry on. The whole crazy structure of war debts and reparations crashed to the ground in 1931-33. It is widely recognized today that this was inevitable; that, indeed, the whole tangle had played a significant part in bringing about the crisis. At the time, however, the action taken by the British was deeply resented by America, as perusal of the contemporary press readily shows. The retaliatory Johnson Act (1934) prevented any foreign government that had not paid its debts from borrowing money in the United States, a provision that was to have considerable significance later. Furthermore, imperial preference became an American bogey and its removal one of the principal aims of State Department policy under Cordell Hull. Thus, at the moment Hitler came to power, America and Britain were further apart than they had been for many years, for, while the naval arguments were fairly abstruse, everyone could understand the simple proposition that the British owed us money and would not pay it.

At the same time, another cause of Anglo-American misunderstanding cropped up in the Far East. The Japanese seizure of Manchuria in September 1931 was followed by the Shanghai crisis of 1932-33. British interests in Manchuria were slight, but Shanghai was the center of British activity and investment in China. There was more British capital invested in Shanghai alone than there was American money in all of China. America, however, had a strong emotional investment in China and deep suspicions of Japan. This crisis might have been the occasion for a display of Anglo-American cooperation that would justify Britain's concessions to the United States in 1919-22 and demonstrate that, even without a formal engagement, America and Britain could work effectively together in the Far East. No such thing happened. Instead it came to be widely believed in the United States that the American Secretary of State, Henry Stimson, had been prepared for strong action against Japan but had been rebuffed by his British counterpart, Sir John Simon. Subsequent research has shown that this interpretation is unfair to both parties. Stimson and Hoover were not as firm, nor Simon as weak, as contemporaries believed, and some later writers have asserted. It is interesting that both sides drew identical conclusions. Stanley Baldwin, the dominant figure in the cabinet, wrote: "You will get nothing out of Washington but words, big words, but only words."[8a] Not only did the Far Eastern crisis of 1931-33 not produce an example of a *de facto* Anglo-American *entente* in operation, it further estranged Britain and Japan. Britain's position was thus worsened in an area where her capacity to defend her interests by force of arms was almost nil, for the Singapore base was not yet complete and British rearmament had not even begun. After the Lytton Report on Manchuria, the Japanese withdrew from the League of Nations, thus sundering another link with the West.

In the six years that remained of peace, British relations

with America seem to have fallen almost into abeyance. The British would not jettison imperial preference or resume payment of war debts. As the European scene darkened, the United States barricaded itself behind a wall of neutrality legislation, as it had barricaded itself in the previous decade behind a tariff wall, whence issued periodic State Department platitudes and Rooseveltian exhortations.

One searches in vain for evidence that Englishmen in that group known as the Establishment, whose views both reflected and shaped policy, thought very much at all about America during the thirties. Harold Nicolson, who retired from the Foreign Office at the beginning of the decade, is a case in point. Nicolson was extremely well-connected—he seems to have spent much of his life having lunch and dinner with the influential. He was, moreover, well acquainted with America. His published diaries are a prime source for British moods and views.[9] One finds there a number of observations about America, some rather trivial, but no comment or speculation on possible joint action in the face of rising dangers in Europe and the Far East. It had come to be accepted that such actions would not occur.

A similar void is detectable in the superb fictional reflection of the Establishment and its fringes found in the second trilogy of Anthony Powell's masterpiece *A Dance to the Music of Time.*[10] The politically committed university students and intellectuals of the thirties looked leftward for the organization of resistance to Fascism rather than westward towards a power that had plainly indicated it had no intention of becoming involved. This feeling is apparent not only in Powell's novels but in Gorowny Rees' recollections of the Cambridge University of his day and in the contemporary writings of George Orwell.[11] America was simply a non-starter in the minds of many appalled alike by the waxing power of Fascism and the feebleness of the British and French governments in combating it.

The same absence of any hope for real help from America is apparent in official circles. The British Ambassador in Washington during these years, Sir Ronald Lindsay, was a former Permanent Under Secretary at the Foreign Office and thus a very senior and experienced career official. But Lindsay was not a man with a political standing of his own in England, such as Lord Reading (Ambassador 1917-18) had enjoyed or Lords Lothian (Ambassador 1939-40) and Halifax (Ambassador 1941-46) later commanded. Nor were there any special missions to Washington like that of Lord Grey in 1919. There was nothing in current Anglo-American relations, or in prospect, that could not be handled by a conscientious senior official like Lindsay. Again one searches in vain for any indication in the published memoirs or personal writings of those connected with Britain's defense planning that they expected anything from America. One officer who served in the War Office during the early thirties and joined the Committee of Imperial Defence in 1938 recalled that everyone had come to expect that, whatever happened, America would not become involved and that there was therefore no point in fretting about it. He added that, even if the British had wanted to take the initiative in proposing consultations, "there was no one to talk to" on the other side of the Atlantic.[12]

Finally, there was a suspicion held by some Englishmen that if America did get involved, the results for England might not necessarily be very happy. Lord Beaverbrook, for example, the eccentric but powerful proprietor of the *Express* newspaper empire, was deeply suspicious of America's ultimate intentions towards Britain. As a Canadian and a passionate believer in the Empire, he felt that a policy of avoiding commitment in Europe (appeasement) was necessary to preserve Britain's freedom to defend her worldwide imperial interests, not least from America.[13] Many other supporters of Chamberlain's policies also included among their mental furniture a few anti-American bits and pieces. Some of this was simply distaste for American society, but, looking back at the sequence of events since the Armistice through British eyes, it is hard not to agree that some of it was based on more solid grounds.

Which brings us to the top of the political pyramid. In the coalition government formed under the impact of the economic crisis of 1931, Ramsay Macdonald, the former leader of the Labour Party, remained Prime Minister, calling himself a "National Labourite," until 1935. The real power in the coalition, however, lay with the Conservatives who held an overwhelming majority over all other parties combined in the House of Commons—the largest majority in modern British political history, in fact. For that reason it is the policy of the Conservative leader, Stanley Baldwin, which has attracted the attention of most historians, although it ought to be remembered that Macdonald, while lacking Baldwin's power, had his uses as a "national" figurehead for an overwhelmingly Conservative government. His views could not be completely ignored—and Macdonald, who had been a conscientious objector during the First World War, loathed the whole thought of rearmament with the corollary that another war might be on the way. Even as a Prime Minister without a political base of his own, Macdonald could exercise considerable powers of delay, and the impression left by officials who had to deal with him on defense issues is that, from a combination of disinclination and failing health, he did just that.[14] It is Baldwin, though, upon whom critics have fastened as the real culprit. He has been consistently pilloried as a man who placed the electoral advantage of his party before the safety of the nation. Recently the record has been adjusted somewhat. While Baldwin can never be completely exonerated, it is now plain that his difficulties were formidable, more so than his early critics appreciated, or at least admitted.[15]

In the first place, Baldwin, underneath the appearance of bucolic stolidity that he liked to project, was a highly strung individual. Like Macdonald, like Neville Chamberlain, like, indeed, every major figure in British political life—except Churchill—the memory of the First World War obsessed him and made him intent upon avoiding what everyone was sure would be a repetition of that bloodbath. (The fact that Churchill seemed immune alike to the scarifying memories of 1914-18 and the fears that the thought of another war aroused, helps to explain why he appealed to so few in the thirties.) Baldwin reflected a widespread public mood—a mood intensified by the fears of what air bombardment would do, fears both mirrored and increased by films like *Things to Come* (1936) which opened with bombs raining down on London. The message was underlined when the

71

Condor Legion obliterated Guernica the following year. Furthermore, Baldwin presided over a divided as well as an anxious country. The government was deeply distrusted by the Labour opposition. It seemed incapable of coping with long-term unemployment or of providing relief on humane terms. It seemed unable or unwilling to sustain the authority of the League or stand up to the dictators. For these reasons the Opposition, although opposed to Fascism, voted consistently against rearmament. It was not a particularly logical stance, but the government had to take account of the emotions that lay behind it.[16]

Finally, Britain's economy and public finances were weak. Massive rapid rearmament would unbalance the recovery from the depression which had begun by the mid-thirties, as well as prejudice Britain's long-term prospects of solvency. To understand what this meant, as well as where the United States fitted in to the picture, it is necessary to look more closely at the state of British defenses and the process of rearmament. From August 1919 until 1933 Britain's armed services had been governed by the "Ten Year Rule"—the assumption laid down by the government that, for planning purposes, the services could assume that there would be no major war for ten years from any given date. This, together with pressure for economy in government expenditure, the prevailing anti-military mood of the electorate, and the hope for a more peaceful future engendered by the League and the "Locarno Spirit," had brought British military power to a very low ebb by 1933. The navy was still one of the two largest in the world, but its heavy units were largely obsolete and no new capital ships would be laid down for three more years. In any case, quite apart from its age, it was not big enough to defend Britain's world-wide interests. The air force was too small, its equipment was obsolete, and it was official Air Ministry doctrine that the United Kingdom was indefensible against hostile bombers. "The bomber will always get through," far from being a measure of Baldwin's faint-heartedness, was merely what his service advisers were telling him. It did little to improve morale. The army was too small and too ill-equipped to do anything but police the Empire, which had been its official function since the end of the First

World War. If Britain was going to fight Germany again, it would have to raise and equip an expeditionary force to fight alongside the French. The latter were unlikely to welcome the idea of having the French army grapple with the Germans while the British defended their Empire, blockaded Germany with their fleet, and bombed German industry (which, according to Baldwin's Air Marshals, was the only way to defend Great Britain from air attack).

In short, the only answer to the strategic dilemma in which Britain found itself—too many commitments, too few resources—was massive rearmament: the simultaneous expansion and modernization of all three services. This seemed impossible in the 1930's. The size of the navy was governed by treaties. The public was not ready for rearmament, which would certainly entail conscription sooner or later. Finally the Treasury, headed by Neville Chamberlain, was adamant that the amount spent for rearmament could not be allowed to reach the point where it prejudiced Britain's economic recovery. This is where America comes in. Massive rearmament would cut deeply into the normal course of trade, particularly the export trade upon which Britain's economic health depended. Furthermore, from a very early stage it was apparent that critical areas of rearmament depended on the ability to buy certain items in the United States.[17] These the British could only get for cash—the "default" of 1933 and the Johnson Act saw to that. The faster the pace of rearmament, the more cash purchases abroad would be necessary. If rearmament ever became uncontrolled, with falling exports and rising outlays, British reserves would rapidly dwindle. This would leave only the alternatives of bringing rearmament to a halt, which would probably not be possible at that point, or of realizing British assets to pay the costs—mortgaging the Empire to the United States—and even to that process there was a limit. This line of thinking was very strong in the Treasury where Sir Warren Fisher, the Permanent Under Secretary, had little faith in American goodwill. Neville Chamberlain, whose business background predisposed him to give more weight to financial considerations than, for instance, Winston Churchill was ever likely to, represented this point of view with great determination in the cabinet. In addition to the normal power a British Chancellor enjoys, Chamberlain was Baldwin's heir apparent as party leader and Prime Minister. As age and fatigue began to loosen Baldwin's grip, Chamberlain, who was no younger but much more vigorous, increasingly became the dominant force in the government. Well before Baldwin's retirement in June 1937, Chamberlain was setting the pace, particularly on defense matters. The only thing that could have cut across this dilemma was an assurance from the United States that British purchases would be facilitated regardless of Britain's ability to pay. Churchill assumed that such would be the case and proceeded on that basis from the moment he became Prime Minister in May 1940. He was proved right—although even he had to pay a high price. By then, however, circumstances were very different. Baldwin and Chamberlain had no expectation that such facilities would be extended to them. They were right—Roosevelt could not have done in 1935, or even 1939, what he was able to do in 1940 after the fall of France and the Battle of Britain.

In the face of all this, British rearmament was governed by what the Treasury would sanction, and what public opinion would tolerate, rather than by what the situation demanded. Under Baldwin progress was slow, and British diplomacy was geared accordingly. The British hoped their rearmament would ultimately have a deterrent effect on Germany, and that diplomacy could perhaps adjust the issues, or at least delay matters, in the meantime. The policy failed, not least (as we can see now with the benefit of hindsight) because it involved a fundamental misconception about Hitler and his aims, but it was neither so purblind, nor so fatuous, as is sometimes claimed. Nor should it be forgotten that it was under the Macdonald-Baldwin regime that the decision was taken that resulted in the development of the radar chain, to which, more than any other material factor, Britain owed its survival in 1940. The two fighter aircraft which will always be associated in the popular imagination with the Battle of Britain—the Hurricane and the Spitfire—were also designed and put into production in the mid-thirties.

There was one issue in particular, however, which Baldwin's government could not successfully resolve (nor could any subsequent British government, including Churchill's). It was less obvious than the failure to confront Germany over her rearmament in 1935 or her reoccupation of the Rhineland in 1936, but in the long run it was even more deadly to Britain's world position. It was also tied to the state of relations with the United States. This was the problem of the defense of the Far East.

Since 1922 the security of the British Empire in the east had rested upon bluff, and the hope it would never be called. The naval base slowly arising from the mangrove swamps on the north shore of Singapore Island was the symbol of Britain's proclaimed intention to send her main fleet east if any threat arose there. Certainly the Royal Navy was serious about the plan. Fuel reserves were assembled at Trincomalee in Ceylon, and the passage of the fleet through the Mediterranean on its way to the Far East was a standard feature of naval exercises in the twenties. The naval war staff had pointed out as long ago as December 1920, however, that an impossible situation would arise if the fleet were needed in Europe and in the Far East at the same time. This was precisely the dilemma that haunted the Royal Navy from the mid-thirties onward. The Germans were rebuilding their navy. The Italians had to be counted as potentially hostile, and Japan definitely was. The only escape here would be an understanding about the Far East with the United States that would leave the Royal Navy free to concentrate on its European antagonists. Many Englishmen had hoped that this would be the consequence of 1922. After all, had they not surrendered their alliance with Japan to please America? There was also the more solidly grounded observation that the United States was hostile to Japanese aims in China. A common foe, it was hoped, would provide the basis for a common understanding. In fact, while the United States was much more active in the Far East than in Europe in the Thirties, it showed no disposition to form a common front with Great Britain there. This brought the British back to the problem of squaring the circle. Given the existence of both a European and a Far Eastern threat, how could they meet both with a navy barely large enough to cope with one hemisphere? The answer was that they could not. This however was not an acceptable answer: there were British interests in the Far East which simply could not be abandoned. There were also Australia and New Zealand, schooled to rely on the Royal Navy as their ultimate security. British policy had to aim at preserving the ability to send a fleet to the Far East. This is turn played its part in two very important episodes of appeasement: the Anglo-German Naval Treaty of 1935 and the Abyssinian debacle of the same year.

In the Anglo-German naval treaty, the British formally condoned Germany's unilateral repudiation of the Versailles Treaty restrictions upon her armed forces by agreeing that Germany could build a navy thirty-five per cent as large as the Royal Navy. Even more surprisingly, the British agreed to a clause whereby the Germans could build up to one hundred per cent of the British tonnage in submarines. The agreement, and the British foreign secretary who negotiated it, Sir John Simon, have been condemned ever since. The French were enraged that the British should so lightly dispose of a matter powerfully affecting French security without apparent concern for anything but their own interests. The verdict of the next four years seemed to establish the treaty as one of the more glaring instances of appeasement. There are several points, however, to be remembered about this episode. The first and most important is that the strongest advocates of the treaty were the Admiralty, headed by the First Sea Lord, Admiral Sir Ernle Chatfield. Chatfield was, by a considerable margin, the most formidable of the British service chiefs of his day and far from the sort of individual normally thought of as an appeaser. Chatfield and his fellow Sea Lords remembered the open-ended naval race with Germany prior to 1914 and were mindful of the problem of the Far East. They were no more prescient about Hitler than most other people. An agreement that limited the new German navy to a permanent inferiority of one to three would leave the Royal Navy with a margin (on paper at least) on which to draw for the defense of the Far East. The British also assumed their new highly secret sonar device had largely negated the submarine menace—this turned out to be an error. Tying down the Germans to an inferior fleet, in a freely negotiated treaty, also seemed timely because complications in the

Mediterranean were adding another fleet to the Royal Navy's potential foes.

It is fortunately not the province of this essay to describe the origin and course of the Abyssinian crisis of 1935. There is only one point about it that is relevant here. The British were concerned in this case also about their margin of naval strength. Even successful war against Italy, if it were to cost several of the irreplaceable capital ships (the British had none building in 1935 and the construction time of a battleship was normally three years), would constitute a strategic defeat in the face of growing German naval strength and an untouched Japanese fleet. In short, should the British risk their already too-slender margin of naval strength in a struggle with a secondary opponent, while her principal enemies, east and west, grew stronger? Moreover Britain had no reliable allies in a naval struggle with Italy. The French had a navy equal to Italy's and almost certainly of better quality, but France, understandably irritated by the Anglo-German naval agreement, was much more concerned with Italian support against Germany in Europe than with the fate of Abyssinia. The British soon discovered that it was by no means certain that even French naval bases, much less the active cooperation of the French fleet, would be made available to them. If the mandate of the League was to be enforced, it would have to be by the British fleet alone. No wonder the prospect daunted Baldwin. His much commented upon remark, that he would never commit the Royal Navy against Italy until he knew what the attitude of the United States would be, reflects the dilemma in which the British saw themselves. They could not chance their arm against Italy lest they subsequently be unable to reinforce the Far East, since they had no reason to expect naval support from any quarter.[18]

The emotion invested in the League by large sections of the British public meant, however, that the British government could not refuse to take some action against Italy. In the end Baldwin got the worst of both worlds. Italian emnity that pushed Italy toward Germany and ended the prospect of sending a fleet to the Far East almost effectively as the loss of several capital ships would have done, as well as the odium of "betraying" the League that

77

alienated voters at home and opinion abroad—these were the consequence of Abyssinia. Churchill may have been right when he argued that it would have been best to leave the whole affair alone, unless the government was prepared to impose its will on Italy. But it would have taken a hardy man indeed to have followed that course in 1935 in the face both of British military weakness and the quite problematic reaction of the electorate.

The Abyssinian crisis leads to several reflections about the relationship between American behavior and British policy during the thirties. The first concerns the League of Nations. Its birth in 1919 had been a joint venture. Furthermore a tremendous amount of emotion had been invested in it, especially in Britain, where the active and influential League of Nations Union focused the energies of League supporters. A very large number of people, in England as elsewhere, made the League the repository of their hopes for a better world order. This made it incumbent on successive British governments to take the League into consideration in shaping their policy—to pay at least lip service to its ideals. Indeed Baldwin won the 1935 general election at least partly on his supposed support for the League, and sank to his lowest ebb in public esteem when the Hoare-Laval Agreement (December 1935) seemed to betray both the League and Abyssinia by reverting to the worst features of the "old diplomacy." Yet the League was always a flawed instrument. The United States remained outside from the beginning. As the skies darkened in the thirties other powers withdrew: Germany and Japan in 1933, and Italy two years later. The withdrawal of three major powers was not really counterbalanced by the accession of Russia in 1934. Baldwin, and even more Chamberlain, distrusted Russia. Although her antipathy to Germany seemed fixed, her utility as an ally seemed much more problematic, particularly after Stalin had decimated the officer corps of his army in the 1937-38 purges. France was concerned only with her security in Europe, understandably in view of the widening gap between her strength and Germany's. What all this meant, however, was that the enforcement of collective security against an aggressor came down to the willingness of the British government to use its armed forces, particularly

78

the Royal Navy, in support of the League. Given the precarious nature of Britain's world position, it is not surprising that the British shied away from the prospect. It is not entirely fair to blame them without at the same time admitting that the absence of the United States from the League left the British to carry an impossibly heavy burden.

Even given America's non-participation in the League, could assurances of support on her part have encouraged Britain to take a firmer stand in 1935? This of course is an unanswerable question. The British knew that it was in the highest degree unlikely that America would give such assurances, let alone live up to them. To that extent, Baldwin's plaint is therefore self-serving, an excuse for inaction. It is also true that Baldwin made little effort to galvanize public opinion into an awareness of the precariousness of Britain's position. Perhaps that sort of candour with the electorate was too much to expect of any British political leader who hoped to stay in office in the thirties. It was certainly too much to expect of Baldwin. When Churchill told the British how dangerous their situation was in 1940, circumstances were very different. His bluntness won him few adherents in the thirties, until events after Munich moved public opinion in his direction. Political leaders are, in theory at least, supposed to lead. Nothing can ever completely palliate Baldwin's failure to do so, but it is necessary always to remember how complex and baffling his situation was. Surrounded by problems of security that were in the last analysis insoluble, and by advisers like Hankey (whose caution stemmed in part from his skepticism about American help), it is no wonder that he hesitated. The events of 1935 are a good illustration of the proposition advanced in the introduction to this essay: the position of the United States helped to establish the parameters of British action. It was a largely negative influence, but an important one nonetheless.

In June 1937 Baldwin retired, and Neville Chamberlain became Prime Minister. Even more than Baldwin, Chamberlain has become the symbol of appeasement. The newsreel footage of his return from Munich has come to stand for all the illusions of the appeasement epoch. Like Baldwin,

Chamberlain was a businessman, and, like him, horrified at the thought of a repetition of the 1914-18 slaughter. There the resemblance ends. Where Baldwin was often woolly, Chamberlain was brisk and decisive. A cold, ruthless, and in many respects unlovable man, he dominated his Cabinet absolutely. The Chamberlain government was much more a one-man show than Baldwin's had ever been. Chamberlain, although he had no experience or background in foreign affairs, soon demonstrated that he intended to manage his own foreign policy, ignoring or bypassing the Foreign Office. He changed both the priorities in British rearmament and the nature of the diplomacy allied to it. Chamberlain did not believe Britain could afford open-ended rearmament and favored the doctrine of "limited liability" advanced by Captain B. H. Liddell Hart, military correspondent of the *Times* and the most influential military commentator of the day. There was to be no "continental commitment," no large British army in France, as in 1914-18, but rather an emphasis on home defense and the protection of trade routes and the Empire. In a war with Germany, Britain's contribution would be a naval blockade and an air offensive with, at most, a token contribution to the front the French would form on land. This was in line with Chamberlain's perceptions of what Britain could afford and where her interests lay, and was not completely unrealistic, especially as Chamberlain did not plan to allow matters to come to the extremity of war. Rearmament was an insurance policy—the underlying causes of European tension would be removed by his personal diplomacy, particularly by the carefully negotiated removal of German and Italian grievances. Thus Chamberlain set out on the single-minded quest for peace that led him to Munich.

As might be expected of a person like Chamberlain, he had a clear perception of where America came into all this. He retained, from the naval arguments of the twenties, a marked distrust of American motivations. In a Cabinet discussion on December 8, 1937, Chamberlain remarked "the Power that had the greatest strength was the United States of America, but he would be a rash man who based his calculations on help from that quarter."[19] One of his "inner circle," Sir Samuel Hoare, later wrote "Rightly or wrongly we were deeply suspicious, not indeed of American good intentions, but of American readiness to follow up inspiring words with any practical action."[20]

For a moment early in 1938 it seemed that things might be otherwise. A tentative approach was made from Washington to London, and Chamberlain brushed it aside. This episode led to considerable controversy in Britain at the time, and it is worth considering what light it throws on British perceptions of America in the year of Munich. Roosevelt's offer (which was to be kept secret until all parties had accepted it) was to convene a conference under his auspices to seek ways of reducing tension. Chamberlain returned a chilling answer without even bothering to consult Anthony Eden, his Foreign Secretary, who was out of the country at the time. Chamberlain feared that such a proposal would upset his own more pragmatic schemes of dealing with the dictators bilaterally and on a case-by-case basis. Eden was very unhappy about Chamberlain's action, and it widened the rift between the two men which was to culminate in Eden's resignation a few weeks later. Not too much ought to be made of this incident, however. Eden and Chamberlain were personally antipathetic (Chamberlain once dealt with a protest from Eden over policy by telling him to go take an aspirin), and Eden resented the way in which the Prime Minister increasingly ignored the Foreign Office. His final break with Chamberlain was more over the tactics of appeasement than the principle, for Eden was never as wholeheartedly a foe of Chamberlain's policy as he came to seem, to himself and others, in retrospect.

Much more interesting is Churchill's criticism. Chamberlain, he felt, should have seized Roosevelt's offer with both hands. It would have served to involve America with Europe, and, if Britain accepted while the dictators refused, it might commit America to further steps. This is certainly what Churchill would have done. The policy of enticing the United States to support Britain, and the associated tactic of getting the affairs of the two countries mingled, was what he did consistently and, aided by events, successfully after 1940. But would it have worked in 1938? That seems much more doubtful. After all, no positive action had followed Roosevelt's Quarantine

Speech (October 5, 1937), and there was no indication that Roosevelt would—or could—secure the alteration or repeal of the Johnson Act or the neutrality legislation, subjects of great concern to the British if war actually came. Chamberlain's action was unnecessarily brusque, but it is very doubtful whether the opportunity Churchill saw was ever actually there. It is worth recalling that, even after the events of 1940-41, it was Germany that declared war on the United States, not the other way around.

The dramatic change that came over British public opinion after Germany seized the rump of Czechoslovakia in March, 1939, dissolved the basis of Chamberlain's policy. Britain promised to support Poland if it were attacked, which Germany did on September 1, 1939. Still the question mark about America hovered over British policy. In February 1940, a leading adviser to the Treasury, Lord Stamp, completed a report on British resources in relation to her war effort for Chamberlain's War Cabinet. In it Stamp pointed out that, at the rate Britain was spending money, her foreign exchange reserves would soon be exhausted. The question, unanswerable at the time, was what would happen then. The caution that characterized British policy during the "Phoney War," so much criticized in the United States at the time, had, as one of its roots, the question about American support that had hung in the air, unanswered, since the thirties began.

On May 10, 1940 the Germans struck in the West, and Winston Churchill became Prime Minister. There was a dramatic change in British policy. On May 15, in his first "Former Naval Person" message to Roosevelt, he told him that Britain would pay as long as she could, but that after that he hoped the Americans would "give us the stuff all the same."[21] Because of the strategic revolution that had occurred between April and July 1940, a way was found. Britain's ability to go on fighting was now perceived as a vital American interest, and public opinion in America had been aroused by the German conquest of western Europe and Britain's lone defiance. The "destroyers for bases" deal in the summer of 1940 and the passage of the Lend-Lease Bill in the winter of 1940-41 brought American aid in abundance to Britain's support. Several points relevant to the theme of this

82

essay ought to be noted about even these events. Though it was now felt to be in America's interest that Britain fight on, the United States drove a very hard bargain, thereby justifying some of the skepticism expressed in the thirties about American goodwill. Even though Churchill successfully resisted the American proposal that the destroyer deal be made contingent on a British promise to send their fleet across the Atlantic if the fall of Britain appeared imminent, the ninety-nine year leases on strategic bits of British territory from Newfoundland to Trinidad in return for obsolescent destroyers of largely symbolic value was hardly an act of excessive generosity. Similarly Lend-Lease, although of tremendous significance for Britain's war effort after 1942, made little difference in 1941, except, again, in a symbolic fashion. The British continued to pay cash for all orders placed prior to the passage of the Lend-Lease Bill, and in the process drained their foreign exchange and sold up many of their overseas assets, while financing the conversion of much American industry to a war footing. The Lend-Lease agreements also severely restricted the maintenance of British export trade during the war, and thereby its revival after-wards. Roosevelt even sent a cruiser to Capetown to collect newly mined gold, despite Churchill's protest that the action might be perceived both by the British public and the world at large as a rapid withdrawal from a failing bank. At the Atlantic meeting in August 1941 the Americans pressed hard for the end of imperial preference. It may be that only measures like this made aid to Britain palatable to large sections of the American public. That is a matter for students of American policy. In any case, the events of 1940-41 hardly justify optimism about what might have been accomplished earlier—or provide any real foundation for a belief in a "special relationship," or the equally long-lived myths that America saved Britain in 1940 and that Lend-Lease was an unselfish gesture.

The story of Britain and America in the thirties has a Far Eastern epilogue far more bitter for Britain than anything that happened in the west. It is with those events that this essay must conclude.

IV

Nowhere was Britain's inability to sustain its own interests and defend the League's principles more palpable than in the Far East. Nowhere would American assistance have been more welcome. The British, as we have seen, had various reasons for hoping that here at least the Americans would make common cause with them. In the late thirties, as Japan plunged into China and made clear her intention of ousting all western interests there, the British government hoped, and maneuvered, for a joint front that would deter Japan, or, if it came to the worst, engage American power in the defense of what they perceived to be mutual interests in the Far East. In this they were wrong. The United States government persistently rebuffed British initiatives—at most Washington would consider parallel efforts by the two powers. Some of this caution stemmed, undoubtedly, from the fear of domestic reactions to joint Anglo-American action, although the very existence of such a fear should have set the British thinking about some of their assumptions. Even more it flowed from a differing view of what American interests were in the Far East. America did not see itself as a colonial or imperial power in Asia. (Whether this view made any historical or logical sense is another question.) American governments certainly opposed Japanese designs and activities in China. That did not carry with it any desire to sustain, or be closely associated with the defense of, an imperial position with which they had no sympathy. When war came the United States was willing to take Australia and New Zealand under its wing, but not the whole of the British Empire in the east.

The British were thus left to align their policy as closely as they could to that of America and hope that if it came to war, America would stand by them. This further exacerbated relations with Japan, although by the late thirties the Japanese were bent on expelling the Europeans from China in any case. More importantly, the British had no real choice. They had been tied to America in the Far East since 1922. By 1937 there was no going back, despite Warren Fisher's desire to "emancipate ourselves from thraldom to the United States and thus free ourselves to establish durable relations with Japan [so that we can] concentrate on the paramount danger at our every threshold."[22]

It is important to realize just how defenseless the British Empire was in the Far East. The Singapore naval base opened early in 1938. By that time it was increasingly doubtful whether its steel and concrete promise would be redeemed by a fleet. A year later Chamberlain told the Australian government, who were naturally anxious about this point, that the despatch of a fleet to the Far East would depend on the situation in Europe. In March 1939 that was cold comfort indeed. With the outbreak of war the "period before relief"—the time that would have to elapse before a fleet from Europe arrived—which had originally been set at forty days, began to rise until it stood at one hundred eighty days. Furthermore it was laid down that the first duty of the authorities in Malaya was to expedite the production of rubber and tin. These were Britain's biggest dollar earners, and, as we have seen, the necessity to pay cash for what was purchased in the United States weighed heavily upon the British for the first two years of the war. This emphasis on "business as usual," unavoidable in the circumstances, was one of the major causes of the military debacle in Malaya when Japan struck.

In June 1940 came the fall of France, which made the despatch of a fleet to the east impossible. It also revolutionized the strategic position in the Far East by opening French Indochina to Japanese penetration, which put their land-based airpower within striking distance of Malaya. Earlier that month Australia and New Zealand had been told that the fleet would not come. The United States would have to look after things in their part of the world.

In 1912 the First Lord of the Admiralty, the thirty-eight-year-old Winston Churchill, had written: "If the power of Great Britain were shattered upon the sea, the only course open to the 5,000,000 of white men in the Pacific would be to seek the protection of the United States."[23] Now in the desperate situation of mid-1940, the sixty-five-year-old Churchill set himself to persuade the United States to underwrite not only Australia and New Zealand but the security of British interests in the Far East as a whole. In the letter to Roosevelt of May 15 mentioned above, Churchill told him

85

that the British were looking to him to keep Japan quiet "using Singapore in any way convenient."[24] This proposal that an American fleet fill the void at Singapore was one to which Churchill was to recur several times, without, of course, any success. Churchill also followed the American lead in relations with Japan. He had no real choice in the matter and, in any case, he believed that a joint Anglo-American front against Japan was the best way to deter the Japanese. Like many in the west, Churchill did not really understand the internal dynamics of the Japanese government. He also believed that if a Japanese attack brought the United States into the war at Britain's side, it would be worth paying whatever forfeits might be exacted in the Far East, since final victory would be assured and anything that was lost would be restored at the end of the day.[25] In the third volume of his war memoirs he recalled the tremendous relief he felt when the news of Pearl Harbor reached him.[26] Seldom was he so wrong. Not in a strategic sense of course, for the Japanese were "ground to powder." But Churchill proved profoundly wrong in his belief that "the Empire would live"—for what he failed to grasp was that the forfeits Japan would exact would be so great as to be irreparable. Above all he was completely wrong in thinking that the United States had any interest in restoring Britain's imperial position in Asia, or anywhere else for that matter.

Intimations that this might be so were not lacking. By midsummer 1941, after the American embargo on oil shipments to Japan, which the British followed and compelled the Netherlands government-in-exile to follow as well in respect of the Dutch East Indies, it was obvious that war was drawing near. The British began to have nightmare visions of a Japanese attack directed solely against them and the Dutch.[27] At the Atlantic meeting, while the Americans pressed him about imperial preference, Churchill sought to elicit some guarantee about the Far East from them. He failed to do so. His declaration that a Japanese attack on America would bring Britain in "within the hour" elicited no American response. It was only on December 5, 1941 that London was able to signal its commanders in the Far East that Roosevelt had agreed that the United States would treat an attack on the British or Dutch in the Far East as an attack upon itself. Forty-eight hours later Japan struck.

News of the American guarantee reached Singapore three days after the H. M. S. *Prince of Wales* and H. M. S. *Repulse* had arrived. These two ships, a new battleship and a vintage battlecruiser, constituted the "Eastern Fleet." Churchill, over-ruling Admiralty advice, had sent the ships east largely as a political gesture. He hoped the ships would help to deter Japan. Although he never said so, he almost certainly expected them to encourage the United States to be more forthcoming by demonstrating that Britain was not merely a suppliant for American aid in the Far East but was ready to make the same vigorous defense of her interests there that had aroused American admiration in the west. On December 10, 1941 both ships were sunk by Japanese aircraft. The shock waves reverberated throughout Asia, for Churchill had been right about the symbolic value of battleships. Their loss was only the beginning of the greatest military disaster in British history. On February 15, 1942 Lieutenant General Arthur Percival surrendered the "fortress" of Singapore, with 85,000 British and imperial troops, to the Japanese. The films of Japanese troops taking possession of the symbol of British power in Asia record the moment when the age of European dominance in the East began to draw to a close.

It is certainly true that nothing the Americans could have done after Pearl Harbor would have prevented the disasters in the Far East. The significance of the episode for this essay lies in the clear revelation of how the British, with resources inadequate to meet their commitments after 1918, let alone after 1940, needed American support if they were to continue to function as a world power. Such support was never likely except on terms that would further reduce Britain's independence. No major power props up another, which it regards with suspicion and rivalry, except for value received. That was the true relationship of Britain and the United States from 1919 until 1941.

V

The conduct of the war after 1941, as has often been

noted, was a remarkable example of a successful coalition in action. This was made easier by the existence of a prime enemy to whose total defeat both partners were dedicated. Roosevelt may have been the first publicly to utter the words "unconditional surrender," but Churchill had vowed to inflict it on Germany in his first speech to the Commons as Prime Minister. It is revealing that the strains in the partnership became greater the more certain victory became. After 1945 there was a brief period when the "special relationship" seemed to flower on both sides of the Atlantic. Memories of a great struggle and victory commonly shared were reinforced by personal friendships formed and mutual respect developed during the war. The British Empire was clearly in dissolution, and Britain had become a subordinate partner rather than one with pretensions to equality. Both of these changes made it easier for Americans to feel benevolent. It seemed that shades of Lexington and Concord had at last been laid to rest. Russia under Stalin provided the equivalent, especially for Americans, of Germany under Hitler; and, in the shattered state of Europe, Britain was the only important ally the United States had. Finally, Churchill worked hard to promote the idea of the "special relationship" for the very hard-headed reason that whatever influence Britain exerted in the world increasingly depended on her ability to shape American views. How far Churchill succeeded is questionable. It is undeniably true that when a real conflict of interests arose at the time of the 1956 Suez Crisis, Churchill's successor, Anthony Eden, discovered how very insubstantial the "special relationship" really was. Many in Britain were genuinely shocked at American action, for they had come to believe that the United States and the United Kingdom really were more than superpower and subordinate.

In the autumn of 1973 Anglo-American differences arising out of yet another of the interminable series of Middle East crises were reflected in editorial comment in Britain pronouncing the special relationship finally dead. It would be more correct to say that a myth, occasionally useful to the British, has finally been discarded with the last remnants of the Empire whose dying days spawned it. At one time its very lack of substance played a role in one of the greatest tragedies in recorded history.

NOTES

[1]I would like to acknowledge the assistance of Mr. W. J. Reader, and Lieutenant General Sir Ian Jacob, G. B. E., with whom I discussed various parts of this essay. My colleague George Basalla made some valuable suggestions. Needless to say, none of them is responsible for what I have written. My wife Mary Helen was, as always, an invaluable editor and critic.

[1a]Quoted in K. Feiling, *Neville Chamberlain* (London, 1946), p. 325.

[2]Committee of Imperial Defence paper quoted in A. J. Marder, *From the Dreadnought to Scapa Flow* (London, 1961-70), I, 183.

[3]Eisenhower to Marshall, April 5, 1943, F. Pogue *George Marshall: Organizer of Victory* (New York, 1973), 189.

[4]The phrase is A. J. Marder's and the best account of it is in his *From the Dreadnought to Scapa Flow*, V, 224-238.

[5]Memorandum by Long of a conversation with [Josephus] Daniels [Wilson's Secretary of the Navy] and Benson, 29 March 1919, Lloyd George Papers F 192/1/4, Beaverbrook Library. By permission of the First Beaverbrook Foundation.

[6]Quoted in M. Beloff, *Imperial Sunset: Britain's Liberal Empire* (New York, 1970), p. 333.

[7]Public Record Office, CAB 2/3, C. I. D. minutes 14 December 1920. By permission of the Controller of H. M. Stationary Office. See also Churchill's remarks on the end of the Anglo-Japanese alliance in *The Grand Alliance* (Boston, 1950), p. 580.

[8]I owe this information to Mr. W. J. Reader.

[8a]Baldwin to Thos. Jones, February 27, 1932, quoted in K. Middlemas and J. Barnes, *Baldwin* (London 1969), p. 729. There is a balanced and detailed study of the 1931-33 Far Eastern crisis by C. Thorne, *The Limits of Foreign Policy* (New York, 1973).

[9]Nigel Nicolson (ed.), *Harold Nicolson: Diaries and Letters 1930-1939* (New York, 1966).

[10]*At Lady Molly's* (Boston, 1957), *Casanova's Chinese Restaurant* (Boston, 1960), *The Kindly Ones* (Boston, 1962).

[11]G. Rees, *A Chapter of Accidents* (New York, 1972). George Orwell's opinions can be sampled in S. Orwell and I. Angus (ed.), *The Collected Essays, Journalism and Letters of George Orwell*. 4 vols. (New York, 1968). The definitive study of Orwell by P. Stansky and W. Abrams has not yet reached the thirties, but Mr. Stansky has told the author that Orwell was not much concerned with America—a reflection doubtless of the fact that America did not seem much interested in stopping Fascism.

[12]Interview with Lieutenant General Sir Ian Jacob, G. B. E., 31 October 1973.

¹³On Beaverbrook's views, see his letter to Churchill of Feb. 20, 1941, A. J. P. Taylor, *Beaverbrook* (London, 1972), 440.

¹⁴See for example Brian Bond (ed.), *Chief of Staff: The Diaries of Lieutenant General Sir Henry Pownall 1933-1940* (London, 1972), pp. 75, 77, 83, 112, 114-115.

¹⁵K. Middlemas and J. Barnes, *Baldwin* (London, 1969). There is a shorter, more readable account by H. Montgomery Hyde, *Baldwin: The Unexpected Prime Minister* (London, 1973). The atmosphere of Baldwin's circle can be sampled in T. Jones, *Diary with Letters* (London, 1954).

¹⁶For the best account of Labour thinking—and voting—on foreign policy and rearmament issues, see John F. Naylor, *Labour's International Policy: The Labour Party in the 1930's* (Boston, 1969).

¹⁷On this very important point, see Correlli Barnett, *The Collapse of British Power* (London, 1972), p. 12.

¹⁸On the naval aspects of the Abyssinian crisis see A. J. Marder, "The Royal Navy and the Ethiopian Crisis of 1935-35" *American Historical Review* LXXV (June, 1970), 1327-1356.

¹⁹Cabinet minutes, quoted in Ian Colvin, *The Chamberlain Cabinet* (New York, 1971), p. 68.

²⁰K. Middlemas, *The Strategy of Appeasement* (Chicago, 1972), 27.

²¹W. S. Churchill, *Their Finest Hour* (Boston, 1949), p. 25.

²²Memorandum of January 30, 1934 quoted in M. Howard *The Continental Commitment* (London, 1972), 87-88.

²³Memorandum by Churchill, January-February 1912. Randolph Churchill, *Winston S. Churchill Companion Volume Two* (Boston, 1969), iii, 1511-1512.

²⁴W. S. Churchill *Their Finest Hour* (Boston, 1949), p. 26.

²⁵Interviews with Sir Ian Jacob, 14 January 1971 and 31 October 1973. Sir Ian was a staff officer to Churchill in his capacity as Minister of Defence throughout the war.

²⁶W. S. Churchill, *The Grand Alliance* (Boston, 1950), pp. 606-607.

²⁷Interview with Sir Ian Jacob, 14 January 1971. See also Churchill *op. cit*, p. 600.

BIBLIOGRAPHY

(An asterisk indicates that a paper edition is available)

The most readable account of Britain during the years covered by this essay is A. J. P. Taylor's *English History 1914-1945* (O. U. P., 1965).* Correlli Barnett's *The Collapse of British Power* (London, 1972) is an extremely important book, to which this essay owes a great deal. The problems of an overstretched empire are very trenchantly analyzed by Max Beloff, *Imperial Sunset: Britain's Liberal Empire* (New York, 1970), which is the first volume of a larger study, and, unfortunately, stops in 1922. There are some interesting reflections on Anglo-American relations in D. C. Watt, *Personalities and Policies* (London, 1965). The recent opening of British official records for the period covered by this essay has produced a number of excellent studies of British defense problems during the interwar years of which two in particular deserve mention: S. W. Roskill, *Naval Policy between the Wars: The Period of Anglo-American Antagonism* (London, 1968) and M. Howard *The Continental Commitment* (London, 1972). Roskill tries to present both sides of the picture but is naturally better on the British point of view; Michael Howard's book is absolutely essential reading for anyone who wants to understand British policy during these years.

Any study of the appeasement years must begin with Winston Churchill's *The Gathering Storm* (Boston, 1949)*, an immensely influential book by reason alike of its author's eminence, the vindication history had seemingly accorded his views, and its wide readership. Its inevitable partiality was less widely recognized and even today it lies at the core of much of the historiography of appeasement. A very different view is found in A. J. P. Taylor's *The Origins of the Second World War* (London, 1961)*, a book which aroused considerable acrimony because of its revisionist bias. A reasonably balanced account is Christopher Thorne's *The Approach of War* (London, 1967). Baldwin's governments have been thoroughly and sympathetically, if somewhat unreadably, examined by Keith Middlemas and John Barnes, *Baldwin* (London, 1969). There is no equally good study of Neville Chamberlain's administration, but K. Feiling, *Neville Chamberlain* (London, 1946), and Ian Macleod, *Neville Chamberlain* (London, 1961) are both useful. The latter tries to say a good word for Chamberlain whenever possible. Ian Colvin, *The Chamberlain Cabinet* (New York, 1971) and K. Middlemas, *The Strategy of Appeasement* (Chicago, 1972) are valuable studies of Chamberlain's foreign and defense policies. Both draw heavily on recently opened British government documents. N. Thompson, *The Anti-Appeasers* (O. U. P., 1971) shows that even later critics of

91

appeasement were by no means consistent in their attitude at the time, in the face of the complexity of the problem. R. Parkinson *Peace for Our Time* (New York, 1971) is largely a paraphrase of the minutes of the more important Cabinet meetings between Munich and Dunkirk, pieced out with material from secondary sources, but it is nonetheless useful. The American reader of all the foregoing will be struck by how little the United States figures in it. On the other hand, L. Thompson *1940* (New York, 1966) gives a good indication of how much the British hoped for and from, American assistance in that memorable year.

On the Far East, the background is in Beloff and Roskill. Christopher Thorne, *The Limits of Foreign Policy* (New York, 1973) is a detailed and balanced study of the 1931-33 crisis in the Far East, that should finally dispose of some hoary myths. N. Clifford, *Retreat From China* (Seattle, 1967) is an excellent account of Britain's unsuccessful attempt to face Japan there, while seeking American support. Two short treatments of the strategy based on Singapore, and its collapse, are found in W. D. McIntyre, "The Strategic Significance of Singapore, 1919-1942. The Naval Base and the Commonwealth" *Journal of Southeast Asian History X* (March, 1969), and R. Callahan, "The Illusion of Security: Singapore 1919-1942" *The Journal of Contemporary History* (April 1974). Both articles have full references. An excellent brief summary of Anglo-American relations during the war is Gaddis Smith, *American Diplomacy During the Second World War, 1941-1945* (New York, 1965)*.

Finally, although rather outside the limits of this essay, no student of Anglo-American misunderstanding should miss Hugh Thomas's study of the last act, *The Suez Affair* (New York, 1967)*.

PERSPECTIVE

The essays that comprise this volume agree on one point, fortunately one of considerable importance. The three major "anti-fascist" powers in Europe gradually lost hope that America would be willing to make common cause with them against the waxing power of Nazi Germany. The closer European war came, the more determined the United States seemed to stay out of it at all costs. Given the state of American public opinion, the Roosevelt administration may well have felt it had no other choice. That is not, however, what these essays are about. What they are about is the effect on the policies of Great Britain, France, and the Soviet Union of their ever-clearer perception that America would engage in nothing except verbal tilts at the dictators. That perception, it is now clear, played a considerable role both in the "appeasement" of Germany by the western democracies and in the abrupt *volte face* executed in the summer of 1939 by the man Winston Churchill once called "Genghis Khan with a telephone." The United States is far from being free of responsibility for the coming of war in Europe. Here, however, agreement ends.

Both Mr. Payne and Mr. Bennett argue (the latter more explicitly than the former) that, while American abstention from European affairs was an important factor in depressing France and alienating the Soviet Union, Great Britain bears the primary responsibility for the failure to contain Hitler. This is a view of quite respectable antiquity, and the powerful authority of Churchill's *The Gathering Storm* can be cited in its support. Now it is undeniably true that the pre-war policy of the British government was a failure. War came. It is also true that of the democracies of western Europe, Britain was the strongest and therefore inevitably cast as the leader. The statement that Britain bears a heavy responsibility thus represents the truth—but far from the whole truth. It is not enough merely to condemn British policy. It is necessary to ask as well why that policy was followed, and whether its architects believed that they had any other choice.

The first point to note is that the containment of Germany

was every bit as much a French as a British interest. (Hitler's expansionism was not in Germany's best interest either, as some Germans recognized at the time, but German attempts to restrain him are notable for their utter feebleness. But this too is another story.) The French felt too weak to do so alone. When a nation feels incompetent to defend what all its leaders are certain is the most vital of its national interests, however, it should be struck from the list of major powers. Poland was a power of the second rank, in all but Polish eyes. Yet it was quite prepared to fight, alone if need be (and, in the event, alone in fact). To some this may prove the fatuousness of Poland's rulers. It also proves that one did not *necessarily* have to have either British or American aid to defend one's most vital interest as a nation—survival. It is difficult to escape from the conclusion that what the French really wanted before 1940 was to be saved from the Germans by someone else—just as, since that date, they have tirelessly sought scapegoats, preferably Anglo-Saxon, for the disaster that overwhelmed them.

That said, it is necessary to turn to what the British did, and why. The British government recognized Hitler's Germany as a potential menace at a very early date. To deal with it required, however, two things: rearmament and a diplomatic strategy. Here the problems began. Rearmament was expensive, and the British government no longer felt rich. Rearmament was also anathema to a very large portion of the electorate. Thus the British government could not move very fast on this front. That it could have moved faster than it did is universally agreed. Baldwin in particular could have done much more to educate the public. But the point here is that it did begin to prepare. Behind much of the criticism of British government could and should have done the impossible: rearmed massively and quickly, and overridden the dominant public mood by committing the country to stop Germany, by force if necessary, at an early date. This simply ignores reality. German designs, while apparent to a well informed or perceptive few as early as 1934, did not produce a decisive change in the national mood until 1938. Before that time British governments proceeded slowly with rearmament. Their diplomatic strategy was tied to this. Under

Baldwin it sought to buy time until British military strength could become a useful deterrent to German ambitions. Chamberlain changed the diplomatic strategy, but even he recognized the need for continued, indeed in some areas accelerated, rearmament. The British government never argued that it could not defend itself unless someone else came to its aid. It set about ensuring that it could at a very early date, and because it did, the weapons needed in the Battle of Britain were ready (but only just). What it did clearly perceive was that it could not simultaneously undertake massive responsibilities in Europe and defend its positions in the Far East, with no assistance except that of an enfeebled France. Here British perception of American intentions was very important. Without American help in the Far East, they had to retain some ability to reinforce that area by limiting commitments in Europe. The only alternative to this was a *rapprochement* with Japan, and this the Americans would not allow. In November 1934 Roosevelt wrote to Norman Davis, the American representative at the upcoming London Naval Conference:

> I hope you will keep two definite considerations always in mind. First, that Simon and a few Tories must be constantly impressed with the simple fact that if Great Britain is even suspected of preferring to play with Japan to playing with us, I shall be compelled in the interest of American security to approach public sentiment in Canada, Australia, and New Zealand and South Africa in a definite effort to make these Dominions understand clearly that their future security is linked with us in the United States. You will know best how to inject this thought into the minds of Simon, Chamberlain, Baldwin and MacDonald in the most diplomatic way.[1]

There was no ambiguity about that. Neither was there any comfort for Britain. Unable to escape Japanese antagonism, except at a completely unthinkable cost, the British government was forced to economize on European commitments. After all it was *British* interests that they had to concern themselves with primarily, an obvious fact but one that often seems to be forgotten. For centuries the British had sought a balance of power on the continent and the independence of the Low Countries. In the 1930s this meant a British determination to keep Belgium, Holland and France out of the German orbit. It did not involve any British commitment in Eastern Europe.

After Munich, and, even more, after Hitler occupied the rump of Czechoslovakia in March 1939, a new factor intruded upon the making of British policy—the arousal of British opinion. Embedded in the body politic of Great Britain is a belief that their country ought to be a moral force in the world. This attitude had often been mobilized before, sometimes with spectacular results, as in the case of Gladstone's great campaign of 1876-77, which was inspired by Turkish repression of a Bulgarian rebellion. After 1918, much of this sentiment had focused itself on the League of Nations Union. While it was doubtless stronger on the left than on the right, it cut across party lines, and permeated all British political life. Once aroused, this force could not be ignored, and the events from Munich to the German occupation of Prague stirred it. Hitler had done what neither Baldwin or Chamberlain had been able, or perhaps desirous, of doing. He had forced upon a deeply reluctant nation the conclusion that something profoundly evil was abroad in Europe, something that posed a threat not only to Britain but to what it stood for in the world. This mood, coupled with the government's strategic concern about a German drive into southeastern Europe, pushed Chamberlain into drawing the line against Hitler in the most unlikely of places. Hitler never understood that *he* had made it impossible for Chamberlain to continue Britain's pre-Munich policy. Nor did he understand that Chamberlain was no longer able to shape British policy entirely according to his own lights.

There is an interesting parallel with recent American history here. Baldwin did not believe he could go farther in foreign affairs than public opinion was ready to sanction. President Johnson essayed precisely this, at a cost that was

96

ultimately ruinous. Chamberlain, like Mr. Johnson's successor, discovered that in the end the weight of national opinion would constrain him to follow a rather unwelcome course.

Furthermore there is a curious "double standard" invoked in judging British and American actions in the thirties. While it is generally recognized that the Roosevelt administration had to walk very warily because of isolationist sentiment, it is often ignored that the length and breadth of the British Isles were dotted with memorials to the dead of the First World War. The mood induced in the British public by that experience has been aptly described by Michael Howard: "there was formulated that simple phrase which the people not only of Great Britain but of the Dominions resolved should be the epitaph of their million-odd war dead: Never Again."[2] The British public was every bit as militantly "isolationist" as the American, and it was the British public that elected British governments. This may have been unfortunate, but it was also a fact of life, and one which critics of British policy in the thirties are all too prone to overlook.

There remains one more specific allegation with which to be dealt. The charge that Chamberlain hoped—schemed—for a Russo-German war, made by Mr. Bennett, is one of long-standing, and also of rather dubious paternity. It was enshrined in a best selling attack on Baldwin and Chamberlain, entitled *Guilty Men*, published in 1940. The author of *Guilty Men* was "Cato," a pseudonym for three Beaverbrook journalists: Frank Owen, the editor of the *Evening Standard*, Peter Howard, his principal leader-writer, and Michael Foot, now a member of Harold Wilson's Labour government. (Beaverbrook loathed Baldwin and was not much better disposed towards Chamberlain.) Like Churchill, Beaverbrook understood the importance of getting one's own version of history on paper first. The charges in *Guilty Men* were repeated in book after book until the opening of the British government records a few years ago allowed historians to examine in detail the formulation of policy during the thirties, and prove them false. Doubtless scholarship will be quite a while catching up with inspired journalism.

Chamberlain and most of his cabinet colleagues were deeply suspicious of Russia—it would have been rather

97

astounding if a Conservative cabinet, whose members had been born when Victoria sat on the throne, had not been. They were moveover convinced that Russia's utility as an ally had been sharply reduced by the purges that had shorn away the high command of the Red Army, an attitude reinforced by the professional advice they received from the Moscow embassy via the Foreign Office. Then there was the simple fact that in March-April 1939 the British government had been forced by circumstances and public opinion to take its stand on behalf of the two powers deemed most immediately threatened by Germany: Romania and Poland. Both these states were strongly anti-Russian, Poland fanatically so. An alliance with Russia certainly seemed to many an obvious necessity if the Polish and Romanian guarantees were to mean anything. Indeed, no group was more convinced of this than the British Chiefs of Staffs, who urged it on the government. Lloyd George and Churchill openly called for such an alliance. But how to achieve it? There was no way to square Russian demands and Polish fears. In the face of this dilemma, should the British government have threatened to revoke their guarantee to Poland (whose military power their service advisors overestimated)? That was hardly likely to discourage Hitler, and was politically impossible in any case. Finally, although the records of British intelligence services remain closed, we do know that the government was being warned by "C"—Admiral Sir Hugh Sinclair, the very anti-Russian head of S.I.S., the Secret Intelligence Service—that Moscow was scheming to bring about an Anglo-German war.

How well or ill Chamberlain handled the March-August 1939 negotiations with Russia is not really important here. The guarantee to Poland had taken control of British policy in Eastern Europe out of British hands, and made an Anglo-Soviet alliance next to impossible to attain. This, not Machiavellian scheming, kept Britain from forming a common front with Russia against Germany. In any case it is rather hard to believe *any* British government would have stood aside and watched Germany conquer Russia, thereby tilting the European balance decisively in Germany's favor and largely nullifying the economic blockade that the British saw as one of their principal weapons in the event of war. Finally it requires a fundamental misreading of the characters of Neville Chamberlain and his principal associates to assume that they were even capable of the degree of "cleverness" that the *Guilty Men* scenario implies. Neville Chamberlain wanted peace, not war, in Europe.

In the end, it all comes back to this. Britain's power was limited by a variety of considerations. Nothing could alter this. The only factor that might have changed the British approach to the challenge of the dictators was a close alliance with the United States. This was an impossibility. Baldwin was not a great leader, but he was clearly what a majority of the British public wanted. So was Chamberlain, until the winter of 1939-40. As Harold Nicolson perceptively noted in the early thirties, Churchill was a man for desperate moments. And only in such a moment could he become Prime Minister. Britain's position in the world and the role it was expected to play, both by others and by many of its own people (perhaps especially by those who were most adamant against rearmament) far exceeded its actual strength. This contributed greatly to the tragedy of the thirties, but it is very hard to see what else the British could have done. In any case, too many of the discussions about the origins of the Second World War have revolved around why the British did not prevent it. The resultant "Munich-fixation" has caused no end of trouble, especially in the United States. Hitler, not the British, bears the ultimate responsibility for the Second World War.

NOTES

[1] Quoted from the Roosevelt Papers at Hyde Park by S. W. Roskill in a letter to the *Times Literary Supplement*, July 26, 1974.

[2] M. Howard, *The Continental Commitment* (London, 1972), pp. 74-75.

[3] D. Dilks (ed.) *The Diaries of Sir Alexander Cadogan 1938-1945* (London, 1971), p. 65. Cadogan was the Permanent Under Secretary at the Foreign Office through which S.I.S. reported to the Cabinet.

THE SOVIET ANALYSIS OF RUSSIAN-AMERICAN

RELATIONS IN THE 1930s

by

Edward M. Bennett

Any attempt to analyze Soviet assessments of American foreign policy in the 1930's must be preceded by an explanation of the peculiarities inherent in the Soviet system and philosophy which dictate certain approaches to foreign policy questions.[1] There is carefully selected publication of Soviet documents from time to time in order to propagandize rather than to inform, but there is no open access to foreign policy documents in Russia even for Soviet scholars. Despite these drawbacks it is possible to trace the pattern and intent of Soviet policy because there is a master plan for setting forth that pattern through the Russian press. Also Soviet leaders desire to make clear to the citizenry their reasons of state that create a certain posture. The task of the Russian statesman is not merely to give public education relative to what is or may be going to happen but to rationalize the government position to the party and the public as they may be distinct from one another.

Vladimir Lenin very frankly expressed the Soviet use of public media as an instrument of the government and the party. Speaking specifically of newspapers Lenin said, "The role of a paper is not confined solely to the spreading of ideas, to political education and to procuring political allies. A paper is not merely a collective propagandist and collective agitator, it is also a collective organizer."[2]

Subsequently Joseph Stalin corroborated and expanded on Lenin's perception of the role of the media:[3]

> The press. . .establishes an imperceptible link between the Party and the working class, a link which is as strong as any mass transmission apparatus. It is said that the press is the sixth power. I do not know whether this is so or not, but that it is a potent one and carries great weight is beyond dispute. The press is a most powerful weapon by means of which the Party daily, hourly, speaks in its own language, the language it needs to use, to the working class. There are no other means of stretching spiritual threads between the Party and the class, there is no other apparatus of equal flexibility.

103

Michael Cherniavsky wrote in his study of Soviet opinion of the United States that all Russian sources are nearly equally valid as they are controlled to the extent that the image being projected emerges as the stated plans of the Soviet leaders and is intended to direct the populace in the view of a policy or a nation.[4] Such uniformity is necessary in the interest of making policy pronouncements appear consistently as the truth and as the word of the constituted authority with which no one may disagree.

Pravda, which is the official organ of the party, and *Isvestiia*, which is the official organ of the government, provide the best sources of both discovering and analyzing Soviet foreign policy in the decade of the thirties. In the same vein these publications were also assumed to be read by foreigners interested in the Soviet posture, and therefore many articles were intended sometimes to educate and sometimes to warn or frighten foreign governments with their perspective and analyses.

Maxim Litvinov, who was Commissar of Foreign Affairs for most of the 1930's, and Stalin frequently ascribed the same motives to Americans which they had for their own actions. As a result they were often confused when the Americans failed to react predictably. Litvinov kept trying to find some hope in the words of Cordell Hull, FDR, or someone connected with the American government which would illustrate that the promises he believed he had secured during the recognition negotiations to block the aggressive designs of Japan and Germany would be implemented.

After several years of anticipating that at last the Americans were about to do something concrete either alone or in concert with the Russians, Litvinov finally remarked to a University of Chicago political scientist, Samuel N. Harper, "Yes. . .we are always expecting more than we should from America forgetting that for a variety of reasons, some of a constitutional nature, America is really incapable of drawing the proper organizational conclusions from its words."[5] Although Litvinov made this comment in 1935, it did not end the expectations of the Russians that the United States would oppose Japan and might even take on Germany as well. Partly this was because Marxist-Leninist dogma predicted a final cataclysmic upheaval among the capitalist-imperialist powers which would bring about their own destruction. Central to this conflict was a clash between the United States and Japan, the two major capitalist powers challenging one another in Asia.

Russians characterized all non-communist states as enemies, but there were degrees of enmity. Some foreign governments could be accepted as more or less friendly enemies because their interests might temporarily coincide with those of Russia in blocking the aggressive course of states which posed a more immediate threat. This was the category into which the United States fell throughout most of the decade. Cooperation with the Americans seemed feasible because American-Soviet interests nowhere came into direct conflict and because the Americans were "glutted" with the conquests of the Spanish-American war which they had not had time to absorb. Also the U.S. was economically powerful and "satiated" relative to the other capitalist states. Therefore, her plans did not call for war, and she could be of assistance to the Soviet peace policy. Because it was Japan which threatened American interests most directly, the U.S. could be counted upon to recognize that the Soviet Union's desire for peace could mesh with the American plans.

Germany was believed to be a secondary threat to the United States, but one which she must recognize. The Americans would have to oppose a dissatisfied power in Europe fomenting a war which did not serve their interest. Thus the two major threats to Russian security were also threats to American interests which would drive the leading capitalist power into a temporary alliance with the Russians. In the American view threats to their interests were not the same thing as threats to their security. This led Russian spokesmen sometimes to attempt to point out to the Americans that national interest and national security were inseparable subjects and, at other times, to try to explain to themselves why the Americans seemed so blind to the realities the Russians perceived. Alternately they suspected that the Americans were simply trying to avoid the whole problem by encouraging Germany and Japan to fight Russia or that the Americans were so removed from the direct menace they were

105

blind to their interests and needed to be enlightened. Whichever course the Russians were inclined toward, and sometimes they inclined towards both at once, they expressed their frustrations in the media and attempted to fathom the "real" American policy.

II
The Search for Friends

For the first two years of the thirties Russian diplomacy largely ignored the Americans. Soviet policy makers smugly pointed to the United States caught in the throes of the depression as illustrative of the evils inherent in the capitalist system. Communists did not believe that the Soviet Union could be touched by the economic chaos sweeping the world. Hitler had not yet come to power on the corpse of the German republic which foundered finally during the flurry of recriminations on war debts and reparations intensified by the economic chaos. Japan's adventure in Manchuria, based in part on the trade problem encouraged by the rising tariff walls resulting from the depression, did not take place until late 1931. Russia's own export-import problems were not yet as affected as they would be, and the Five Year Plan was still believed to be a panacea which did not rest on external stimuli. The diversion of resources to meet the needs of defense against rising menaces on the extremities of the Russian borders had as yet been only dimly foreseen.

To be sure there were Soviet thrusts concerning the folly of the Americans in not recognizing the reality of the existence of a Soviet Russia. There were both prominent and obscure Americans quoted on the degree to which it was indeed folly not to take advantage of the opportunities of a Russian market in time of economic difficulties. But there was no campaign for recognition such as that which would be mounted when the opportunities for such action seemed more imminent and the need more imperative. In 1932 a general campaign began in the Soviet press to conjure recognition from the United States. While it may be considered natural to desire recognition and to quote anyone to the effect that it should come, the Russian press campaign focused on the need for it on the part of both the Soviet Union and the USA in the interest of preserving the peace.

On March 16, 1932, Tass, the Soviet news agency, released a story in *Izvestiia* with a London dateline citing external sources, "Well informed London circles are watching with interest information from Washington to the effect that the Government of the United States will perhaps, in connection with conditions in the Far East, alter its position with regard to the Soviet Union."[6] The implications of this development were clearly asserted, "It is pointed out that the Washington circles do not deny that the United States would like to see the USSR strengthened so as to establish, through recognition of the Soviet Union, a balance of power in the Far East." Not only did this intend to relay the changing perspective of the American government but also that the Soviet Union had the same results in mind as the writer continued, "According to the reports, Washington circles also believe that the Soviet press, reflecting the policy of the Kremlin, has recently adopted a friendlier attitude toward the United States."

Japan's attack on Manchuria on September 18, 1931, turned Russian fears of an aggressive Japan into reality. U.S. support and identification of interests with the Soviets became more important than ever before, for now the Japanese Army had a foothold in a satellite state bordering directly on Russian territory. *Pravda* became more insistent that the developing struggle in Asia involved the United States. On January 7, 1933, *Pravda* quoted the *Shanghai Evening Post and Mercury* to the effect that after Japanese occupation of Manchuria the positions of the U.S. and Japan were irreconcilable, and if Japan continued her aggression in China she would have to fight the United States. Two weeks later on January 21, quoting the New York *Herald Tribune*, *Izvestiia* foretold a growing determination in the U.S. to take a stronger posture in Asia and to oppose Japanese objectives. The writer asserted that a firmer position was expected from the Roosevelt administration than had existed under Stimson's direction.

Franklin D. Roosevelt did indeed have plans to bring Japanese aggression under control. The Russians fitted into those plans, but they were not as clearcut in terms of direct action as the Soviets anticipated. The first move was taken while FDR was President-elect in the form of a secret trip by William C. Bullitt to Europe. Bullitt and the President-elect assumed that Japan was in poor condition to continue her aggression without financing, and therefore one of Bullitt's tasks was to make sure that neither England nor France permitted the Japanese to get loans in their countries. Bullitt cabled FDR that he was assured by Prime Minister Ramsay Macdonald and Premier Paul-Boncour that no loans would be given to Japan.[7]

A Tass representative in New York was able to provide a story which further strengthened the Russian conviction that a turnabout had to come soon. Quoting Raymond Leslie Buell, the director of the Foreign Policy Association, from the *New York Times* the reporter observed in *Izvestiia* on January 24 the problem which confronted the U.S. in her Far Eastern policy because she did not recognize the Soviet Government. Buell had told a *Times* correspondent that "American policy in the Japanese-Chinese conflict displayed the embarrassment created by nonrecognition of the Soviet government. The League of Nations and the USA are not able to calculate on success, while they abandon the side of the USSR which forms the third side of an equilateral triangle." This article followed by one day a lengthy report by V. M. Molotov to the Central Executive Committee of the Party on the current status of Soviet foreign policy. In his assessment Molotov told the committee that the internal situation must remind them of the need for increased vigilance especially in the Far East. He concluded with a warning, "This must be reflected in all our work and in everything we are building, for that is the foundation of our economic and political power." Molotov's address was given a very detailed editorial analysis in *Izvestiia* where the point was made that the United States figured quite prominently in current Soviet foreign affairs. The year, according to Molotov, had "...reinforced in the United States the tendency toward recognition of the USSR." The enticements which made this change in attitude were spelled out by Molotov in terms of the Americans finally realizing that the Soviet Union was a political reality, that its trade was desirable and stable in a time of economic crisis, and that the Americans recognized they were losing the opportunity to cooperate with the Soviets in the interest of preserving the peace. He then scored Germany indirectly and Japan directly for their unwillingness to pursue a peaceful policy, warned that Russia would not be taken unaware or unprepared, and reiterated the Soviets' position because they were not duped by German and Japanese pretensions.

American policy was said to be "cloudy," but an *Izvestiia* correspondent professed to see a hardening of lines relative to Japan because of treaty violations, presumption of American interests in Asia, and insults to American prestige which could not be tolerated by a major power. Republican newspapers were reported as rejecting the cautious Hoover policy and supporting a more forthright challenge to Japanese imperialism beginning with expansion of the fleet. Anticipation of support against Japan was clear as the *Izvestiia* writer observed:[8]

> At any rate Roosevelt's support of Stimson cannot be discussed in the sense that the new administration will tend to repeat the alluring gestures in the open diplomatic arena. . . . The impression is becoming stronger that the policy of the new administration will be more flexible and more "realistic." This policy perhaps to a unique degree will forego the demonstrative gestures of Stimson's type as well as the conservative passivity of Hoover and the circles closely connected to him. It might refrain from seeking its goals so insistently yet do so with patience. However, the traditions of the Democratic party to a certain degree demand that its leaders act—although in a less ostentatious manner than Stimson—in defense of general principles and the inviolability of treaties.

The Russian view of American policy was one of concern and hope, for if the Americans with their vast economic and potential military power were convinced that there must be no war there would be a delay which could only assist the

USSR. The problem was to fathom the United States' concern and encourage a firm position toward the prospective enemies and if possible gain commitments of assistance.

Meanwhile the Americans were considering the two unfriendly neighbors of Russia and what, if anything, ought to be done about them. FDR gave substance to the fear that Germany was preparing to create a new war. In April in response to the question, "What is the likelihood of war with Germany?" FDR told Secretary of the Treasury Henry Morgenthau Jr., "A very strong possibility." Morgenthau asked if the United States would have to go in to defend her treaty rights, and the President responded, "We don't have to send any men abroad anyway."[9]

President Roosevelt's concern about the growing aggressiveness of Japan and the inclination of Germany to disregard the provisions of the Versailles Treaty became general knowledge in what the Soviet press liked to refer to as "high Washington circles." This information fed Soviet belief that at last the United States had no choice but to renew relations with Russia in her own interest. Thus when FDR called for the signing of nonaggression pacts among all the world powers on May 20, 1933, an *Izvestiia* writer imputed a special significance to his request. The *Izvestiia* writer saw the move as aimed most specifically against Germany because "fear of European complications has increased lately in Washington circles." The fear was supposedly connected to an expected German repudiation of the Versailles Treaty. The President of the United States was expected "...more and more...to support the status quo," and he would "show beforehand who bears the blame [for threatening the peace] before the entire civilized world." The Russian judged the fact that an invitation was sent to unrecognized Russia was important. While he thought the move important because it focused attention in the isolated U. S. on foreign policy, he judged the content of FDR's message to be unrealistic and Wilsonian.

The specific importance of FDR's message to the USSR was pointed out by *Izvestiia* on May 21. Here at last was a capitalist power with which the USSR could cooperate. The U. S. agreed with the proposal for arms limitations and would

110

go further in suggesting disarmament because she agreed with the objective of denouncing economic exploitation of one power by another and approved of round-robin nonaggression pacts. The United States would probably find, however, that only the Soviet Union would agree to really support Roosevelt's proposals, and he would be disappointed in the reactions of those nations socially closer to the Americans.

Russian hopes were intensified relative to prospects for cooperation in keeping the peace as reports of the American reaction to the Soviet response to FDR's message poured in. On May 22 *Izvestiia* quoted American newspapers illustrating the theme that the Soviet answer to Roosevelt was evidence of a rapprochement between the two nations. Most papers quoted gave praise to FDR for recognizing that the USSR, "like it or not," was an enormous military and economic power in the world.

While the Russian press was approving FDR's proposals but judging them naive, the President illustrated an unusual analysis of the general response. Relative to his message to fifty-five nations he asked Henry Morgenthau, Jr. what he thought of it. Morgenthau thought it changed the whole situation in Europe, and FDR agreed. "I think I have averted war," said the President.[10] Roosevelt's high expectations for his move would hardly have been taken seriously in the USSR. The Russians saw other significance in the message, whose purpose they thought secretly might be directed toward them.

The more threatening the relationship between Japan and Russia became the more fervently the press predicted the coming conflict between the United States and Japan. There were two reasons for this connection: The Russian leadership hoped to convince Japan and the United States that they were primary enemies, and they hoped to convince the Americans that the mutual enmity dictated a rapprochement. In this campaign there appeared in the press during September numerous articles quoting Japanese concerns and threatening posture relative to the United States and vice versa. Stretching a point to illustrate American preparation to meet Japan did not deter the Soviet writers as *Pravda* noted on September 23 a sixty four million dollar appropriation for the Civilian

Conservation Corps which was reported in the Russian press as an expenditure taken from the Public Work Funds for construction of "military barracks."

It was during the period after July 1933 that the Soviet drive to convince both Russians and Americans of the mutual benefits of renewing relations intensified. Such a campaign existed before with varying degrees of intensity, but it began to appear more insistently as a likely prospect during the months after June. The reason for this prediction came as a result of American initiative towards recognition. FDR told Morgenthau in July that he wanted him to get in touch with Boris Skvirskii, who represented the American Trade Organization of the Soviet Union in the United States (Amtorg), and along with William C. Bullitt, Roosevelt's Russian expert, find out how the Russians would receive overtures towards renewing relations.

It was small wonder that the Russians became excited for those oft quoted "highest Washington circles" buzzed with rumors that impending recognition was aimed at stopping Japan directly and dealing with Germany subsequently. A new phase in the Soviet-American relationship seemed apparent.

III

Anticipation of Rapprochement

Pravda and *Izvestiia* both reported significant signs of a Soviet-American rapprochement on September 30, 1933. *Pravda* observed that according to "information from authoritative sources," FDR had recently begun personally to study all of the commercial and political questions regarding the Soviet Union. The predicted result according to "several prominent industrialists in Washington" would be consideration of the question of policy in relation to the USSR. Actually the *Pravda* writer was in error for Roosevelt had been examining the pros and cons of recognition since before his inauguration and moved only after he decided that most of the media and public opinion generally would support recognition.[11] *Izvestiia*, although it reported the same facts as *Pravda*, put it in a more promising context for Soviet foreign

112

policy. The spokesman for government opinion recorded that Roosevelt had personally taken charge of "all matters commercial and political concerning the Soviet Union" and that this meant a new relationship was not doubted. *Izvestiia's* sources asserted that Morgenthau had been placed in charge of commercial and political relations with the Soviet Union in order to eliminate confusion which meant that the general tone of the relationship was becoming more open. While touting the significance of the new relationship between the United States and the USSR, *Izvestiia* related on October 9 that the Americans were taking a harder line against Germany.

With the knowledge that recognition by the United States might and probably would be forthcoming the Russians intensified their campaign to illustrate the irrepressible conflict that was building between the United States and Japan and at the same time subtly inserted the USSR into the affair. At this juncture Japanese statesmen aided the Russian predictions. Prince Konoye, Chairman of the Upper Chamber of the Japanese Diet, warned, according to a *Pravda* report of October 1, that Japan was arming because the United States was expanding her Pacific fleet and that any attempt to establish naval supremacy in the Pacific on the part of the Americans would "be the signal for a clash between the USA and Japan."

Soviet expectation of a more positive policy emanating from Washington gained credence when on October 15 *Izvestiia* capsulized Roosevelt's speech in which he said that the United States wished to renounce seeking territory by conquest "and those countries that are seeking territorial aggrandizement are leading the world into war." To recognize such a possibility without doing something about it seemed inconceivable to the Russians. Such expectations of American action appeared warranted when on October 16 *Izvestiia* communicated Cordell Hull's "firm statement" after Germany's withdrawal from the League, "Germany's action definitely halts any further steps toward disarmament."

What the Soviets hoped to gain through recognition was reported by the American chargé d'affaires ad interim in Riga, Latvia. His assessment was very close to the mark. The Russians wished recognition to be identified with their plans to insure the preservation of peace. Whereas the Soviets usually tried to sell the benefits of commerical relations through recognition this now dropped to an insignificant position. Although Japan was not mentioned by name as being affected by recognition, "stock Soviet phrases which were consistently in use as references to Japan were included such as 'groups of irresponsible adventurers' and 'adventurous predatory plans.'" The chargé explained that these phrases were also used in reference to the Nazis but less frequently at that particular time. He made another observation on Soviet objectives. He believed that the reference to closer relations being welcomed by all friends of peace could be taken as a reference to matters pertaining to the Far East "since that is the most immediately obvious field for any coordinated action of policy between the two countries." The chargé observed that to make common cause against Germany was a subject that was not of pressing importance and was in the background in the minds of the Soviet leaders while Japan was in the foreground. He ended his despatch with this observation:[12]

> ...all of the Soviet comment on the President's message stressed its contribution to peace throughout the world and the veiled references to Japan... as well as the direct references to American-Japanese rivalry in the Pacific, the Far East, Asia, and the Chinese Eastern, all taken together justify the conclusion that the Moscow press is making an attempt to represent the President's initiative to the Soviet public as an offer of moral, or even more concrete, support by the United States for the U.S.S.R. against Japan.

Obviously the Russian hopes for results in blocking Japanese expansion in Asia were well understood in the Department of State. Since copies of the despatch went to the Division of East European Affairs and Assistant Secretary of State R. Walton Moore, it was not likely that there could be any misreading of Soviet objectives when Maxim Litvinov traveled to Washington to negotiate for recognition.

114

Russia's fervent desire for recognition was understood in intent, and the President and the Department of State attempted subsequently to use this knowledge to gain payment of the debts owed by Russia to the USA but did not wish to pay anything more for them in diplomatic currency than recognition itself. The Soviets on the other hand expected recognition merely as a first link in a chain of events which would result in the United States taking the lead against Japan or providing proof to the Japanese that there was a firm agreement that each state would stand with the other against further aggression. The Russians did not anticipate a leading position from the United States where Germany was concerned but did expect here too that she would not be left adrift in the face of a German onslaught because the United States could not desire another European war which would affect her interests. The basic problem was the Russian inability to understand where the United States would draw the line in the understanding of her security problems. The remainder of the 1930's were to be spent in trying to comprehend the American position and to react thereto in Russia's best interest.

Not only did the Russians expect and hope for more from the United States than they received, but they believed by their own analysis that there were positive signs that they *should* expect more. *Izvestiia* illustrated Russian hopes many times by coupling articles which, as the Soviets viewed it, should lead to what Litvinov had described to Samuel Harper as "proper organizational conclusions." When the Soviets discovered that the United States emphatically refused to accept an exchange of good-will missions with Japan, they rejoiced. When the American press favored recognition and predicted an effective move by the two powers to calm the troubled water in Asia, the Russians believed this was an American warning to Japan, and if one power warned another then something concrete would have to follow.

While the Russians hoped for such a reaction people like Stanley K. Hornbeck in the Department of State's Far East Division feared that the Roosevelt administration might make such a move. When in October it became fairly obvious that recognition would come, Hornbeck, who consistently took an anti-Japanese posture in the thirties, wrote one of his famous position papers for the Secretary of State which he wanted circulated throughout the government. He advised that the technique to be followed by high government officials in answering questions about what the United States expected from Soviet recognition talks should be to avoid discussing anything relating to the Far East with Soviet delegates.[13]

What the Americans planned to do about worrying Japan was therefore questionable, but for the Russians there was no doubt. As recognition approached, the Russian posture toward Japan became stiffer. The Soviets spoke bluntly in terms of preparing for war if the Japanese did not recognize Russian rights in Asia or if they attempted to "steal" the Chinese Eastern Railway.[14]

When the recognition agreement was announced after the official signing on November 16, 1933, the Soviet press campaign to impress the significance of this event on the world and especially on Japan and Germany intensified. *Pravda* and *Izvestiia* liberally quoted what foreign newsmen had to say about recognition relative to keeping the peace in Europe and Asia. Accompanying the world assessment was an attempt to make a very close relationship with the United States palatable to those who had been led to view all capitalist powers as enemies.

Maxim Litvinov made absolutely sure before he left the United States that no one misunderstood the significance of renewed relations between the USA and Russia. For those who might suspect Soviet motives he attempted through a speech in New York City to give an impression of the obviously similar characteristics between the two giant peace loving countries. He charged that it would be difficult to find anyone who believed that the World War was the last war. The evidence of preparation for a new war was everywhere evident amongst nations that propagandized their peoples on the glories of war and where songs, music, popular epics, literature and science were made subservient to militarism. Without naming them Litvinov made it clear that the breakers of the peace would be Germany and Japan. After identifying the enemy and the obviously virtuous nations, he concluded:[15]

What is still more important, can any question now
arise as to whether both the United States and the
Soviet Union will benefit from the joining of their
efforts in the cause so important to both of them—
the great work of preserving peace? Who can doubt
that the combined voices of these two giants will
make themselves heard and that their joint efforts
will weight the scale in favour of peace?

Litvinov's hope relative to cooperation in the security field
was expressed on the way home to newsmen wherever he
appeared. The theme was picked up in the Soviet press and
hammered home for those who needed convincing. The
Russians rejoiced when Roosevelt's special advisor on Soviet
affairs was appointed as the first ambassador to the USSR.
William Christian Bullitt was advertised as the ideal man for
the job, for he was known as a fair observer of the Russian
way of life which in Soviet jargon meant that he was thought
to be sympathetic. The Russians were later to regret their
assessment of Bullitt. When he left the country in 1936 for a
new assignment, he was termed a fascist brigand. The Russian
foreign office was moved to wish, after watching Bullitt's
growing disillusionment with the great experiment in Russia,
that the Department of State would send them no more
sympathizers and idealists but rather some hardheaded Wall
Street capitalist with whom they could deal on a realistic
basis and who would have no illusions about Russia to be
shattered.

While Bullitt was in full favor early in his tenure he was
very quotable from the Russian perspective. However, they
did not always really understand what he was saying, and this
had nothing to do with a language barrier. When in December
1933 *Izvestiia* quoted a speech by the American ambassador it
was crammed into Russia's framework of collective security
cooperation between the USA and the USSR. Bullitt said that
the will to peace was the way to peace, and both countries
wanted it. Since both were giant powers, who could withstand
their thrust for peace? The Russians chose to convey the
belief that this meant that real cooperation for preserving the
peace would be forthcoming such as joint pressure on Japan

and Germany, collective security agreements, nonaggression pacts, friendly visits of the American fleet to Russia in order to impress Japan, and similar cooperative gestures. What Bullitt actually meant was that the combined moral pressure of the two giants could not be resisted by the rest of the world. The *Izvestiia* article was too obvious in its assessments of the meaning of Bullitt's address as the title indicated— "Friendship Between USSR and USA Is a Guarantee of Peace."

Meanwhile Bullitt was outlining for Hull the high value the Russians placed on American moral support. The ambassador was pleased that Litvinov asked him before the fact if the United States would object to the Russians surrendering to French pressure to join the League of Nations before a mutual security agreement with France was signed. When Bullitt asked why this was important, the Commissar of Foreign Affairs responded that the French had asked for a regional agreement for defense against attack by Germany with each party to declare war on the Germans if the other were attacked by them. This was judged necessary because the Russians were convinced that the Japanese were going to attack them in the spring of 1934, and they believed that there was an arrangement between Germany, Japan, and Poland against the Soviet Union. The Russians did not expect that Poland and Germany would join in unless the war dragged on for two years, but Litvinov felt that the western borders had to be secured in any event.

Bullitt was puzzled by French insistence that the Soviets join the League as part of this agreement. Litvinov explained that the French thought this would enable them to evade the difficulty created by the Locarno agreements. The agreement between France and Russia would then be introduced to the League as a regional understanding and therefore permissible. Bullitt said there was a considerable region between France and Russia, but Litvinov countered that the proximity of both powers to the Germans would make it acceptable. Bullitt foresaw the expectations that the Russians might have relative to American assistance. Thus he informed the President and the Secretary of State:[16]

I repeatedly emphasized to all with whom I talked that the US had no intention whatsoever of getting into war with Japan but that our participation in any Far Eastern difficulties would be confined to the use of our moral influence to maintain peace. Nevertheless the Soviet Union is so anxious to have peace that it is obvious that even our moral influence is valued very highly by the Soviet Government.

This was a far cry from the significance of the new relationship between the United States and Russia which Litvinov explained to the French ambassador to the United States, André de Laboulaye. The ambassador reported to his Foreign Minister a conversation with Litvinov just after recognition had been accorded by the United States. The Russian told Laboulaye, "It was the political consequences of the recognition that had a real importance. All the rest, he said, must be considered as only secondary." Litvinov went on to explain that the demonstrated will of FDR to work for peace and his worry about Germany and Hitler opened up to the USSR "perspectives of a commonality of Russian-American action which have visibly cheered him up." The Frenchmen also said that Litvinov expressed the hope that France would be associated to this peace policy since FDR, during his talks with the Russians, seemed especially well disposed toward France.[17]

In other ways the Russians were convinced that the areas opened for close cooperation were many and profitable from a security standpoint. Louis Fischer, who had firsthand contacts with the Russians, wrote an article for the *Nation* which purported to give the real motives behind recognition. The important thing according to Fischer was the opening of Department of State archives to show Litvinov a number of documents "proving that Woodrow Wilson sent General Graves with troops to Siberia in 1918 not to fight the Bolsheviks but to check the imperialistic plans of Japan on the Asiatic continent." Accordingly Fischer concluded, "It must have been clear that the Commissar would put only one interpretation on the opening of its files: that Washington

was still anti-Japanese and wanted Moscow to know it. . . .
President Roosevelt knows that in most other respects, too,
Russia's attitude toward Far Eastern affairs is very much like
his own." Fischer found irony in the Far Eastern situation
where Communist Russia seemed destined to "guard the
capitalist system from a serious body blow in Eastern Asia.
Communist Russia must do it, and capitalist America will
assist her in doing it."[18] In some degree if this view was
being expressed by Louis Fischer his close contact with
Litvinov assured that the Russians understood the situation
this way.

Part of the difficulty the Russians experienced with
American policy makers was the way in which FDR and Hull
expressed their preferences in the foreign affairs area.
Continuously the Soviets were led to believe that something
significant was happening because pronouncements from
Washington seemed to be taking a more belligerent attitude
towards the potential aggressors. Then the new toughness
would be softened by another bland statement which left the
Russians wondering. In his State of the Union message in
1934 FDR asserted, "Unfortunately I cannot present a
completely optimistic picture of the international situation."
He followed this with a warning that despite the desire to
seek peace and disarmament the expenditures for increased
armaments continued along with trade barriers and these
things were threatening war. He promised to continue to work
against these dangerous trends. *Pravda* repeated the message
on January 5, and the Russians again thought that they saw a
realist in control of American policy. *Pravda* was only too
happy to report on January 7 that a leading Japanese newspaper *Asahi* viewed FDR's speech as dove-tailing with a
similar statement by Molotov to the Communist Party on the
same day and that the Japanese thought the two addresses
were aimed specifically at them.

When Alexander Troianovskii arrived in Washington to
assume his duties as Russian ambassador his first interview
with the press was described by *Pravda* on January 12, 1934,
as cordial. The fact that he was questioned relative to the
relationship between the Soviet Union and Japan was
emphasized. Troianovskii stressed, as did other Russians in

this period, the importance of the new relationship between his country and the USA as a force working for peace and stability in the world.

Russian objectives and expectations relative to the relationship to the United States really had little relevance as a basis for policy unless approved by Joseph Stalin. The final word relative to the meaning of recognition was expressed by Stalin at the Seventeenth Congress of the Communist Party of the Soviet Union on January 26, 1934. Stalin told the group that a new war was being planned, and the Soviet Union was the chief target of many of the plotters against the peace— especially Germany and Japan. There were numerous reasons why these plots could not succeed. With involuted reasoning he pointed out the attacks by German and Japanese propagandists on the USSR to illustrate the reality of the danger, but Soviet planning had weakened their position because the people supported the Soviet peace policy. The Russian army was strong and the restoration of normal relations with the United States which had previously been in the enemy camp was very important.[19]

> There cannot be any doubt that this act is of great significance for the whole system of international relations. It is not only that it improves the chances of preserving peace, and that it improves the relations between the two countries. . .and creates a base for their mutual collaboration. The point is that it is a landmark between the old position, when in various countries the U.S. was regarded as the champion of every kind of anti-Soviet trend, and the new position, when the championship has been voluntarily dropped, to the mutual advantage of both countries.

Here the direct connection was made between the joint policies of the USSR and the USA vis-à-vis Germany first and Japan second for one of the few times in the immediate post-recognition era, and it was made by the real force in Russian policy making.

At the same Party Congress War Commissar Marshall Klimenti Voroshilov spoke, and it was his task to emphasize

Japan almost to the exclusion of Germany. It was also his responsibility to reiterate the significance of new alignments in the world relationship. He too emphasized that Russians could not afford to be complacent in the hostile world that surrounded them but that their policy was winning the battle of diplomacy for they were the agents of peace for the whole world.

The new thrust of Soviet policy was made clear to Louis Fischer by his inside contacts. He then wrote a feature article on the subject for *Fortnightly* which again placed the heaviest emphasis on the Soviet-American friendship and its effect on Germany. Fischer assessed the Soviet Foreign Minister, Litvinov, as a "rugged realist" who was charged with the responsibility of leading the move toward "co-existence" with the United States. Fischer said that this was the first clue to the Soviet Union's new foreign policy. The second was Moscow's new antagonism towards Germany and its move toward an alliance with the French. The new view facilitated rapprochement with America and France. Fischer saw a direct connection between Russo-German antagonisms and American recognition. Equally he saw the same relationship between the rapprochement and Japan. He did not agree with Russian predictions that Japan would attack the USSR in the spring of 1934. Fischer thought it was already too late for such an attack to be effective, for the Russians had mended their fences both militarily and diplomatically in the Far East. Where Far Eastern fence mending was concerned the United States had played a crucial role: "Whether President Roosevelt intended it or not—and he may have—recognition has been interpreted as a friendly gesture towards Moscow's stand in Pacific affairs."[20]

Opinion in the United States and the Soviet Union focused after the recognition event on the happy results which were supposed to follow. Eagerly the Americans began to press for payment of the Russian debts in order to have proof of Russian good faith. At the same time in hope of cementing the partnership and to forestall a Japanese attack the Russians immediately began to press for a bilateral nonaggression agreement. The results were not auspicious for the plans of either power.

122

IV

Developing Suspicions

Early phases of the Soviet-American relationship after recognition led to some disgruntlement on both sides and some speculation by each government as to the peculiarities of the other. Generally, however, there was still a hopeful attitude prevailing concerning the working out of mutual disagreements and cooperating in creating a more peaceful world. This hope lasted much longer on the part of the Soviets than the Americans.

Cordell Hull and William Bullitt were concerned more with getting the Soviets to pay their debts assumed from the Kerensky regime agreed to in the recognition negotiations than working on any arrangement to draw closer to the USSR in her efforts to thwart Japanese aggressiveness. The Bullitt-Hull correspondence and Bullitt's exchanges with Assistant Secretary of State R. Walton Moore are replete with plans to force payment by threatening the Russians with a diminution of cooperation and the cessation of moral support unless the debts were paid.

After predicting that the debt question was not insoluble Bullitt ran up against a brick wall which he ascribed to an improvement in the Soviet-Japanese relationship. The degree to which Bullitt both understood and misunderstood the Russian perspective simultaneously is remarkable. He thought the Russians were playing games with the Americans on a selfish basis of narrow national interest. They would not live up to their obligations he informed Hull "unless they need us." Bullitt's idea under the circumstances was to bluff the Russians with the threat of a closer relationship to Japan. He suggested that the Russians be told, "We want to work intimately and cordially with you, but if you do not want to work with us we shall work with those who do wish to work with us." He thought that "a mere hint" in the direction of giving to Japan the services of the Import-Export Bank set up to do business with the Russians would "produce agreeable results."[21]

Bullitt expressed here what might be termed the arrogance of isolationism. It was all basically a one-sided view of cooperation. The Russians must be honorable and pay their debts, and the Americans in their benevolence might condescend to do something nice for the Russians in the way of moral support against a Japanese attack or to continue to let Japan guess about the Soviet-American rapprochement. The Russians on the other hand did not believe that they should pay for a pig in a poke. If the Americans were not going to do anything more concrete than restore normal relations, they were not going to pay for it when they were convinced that recognition had been unjustly withheld in the first place.

Soviet leaders were prepared to pay the debt if the United States would provide them with unrestricted loans or unrestricted credits in an amount equal to the debt. In this way no other Soviet creditor nations could afford to demand an equivalent settlement. The Soviets argued that the terms of repayment had included discussion of loans and credits, which they had, but they also very well knew that credits were intended to be used for purchases only in the United States and not to be unrestricted. The interesting point here was that just as Bullitt and Hull thought to use the offer of closer cooperation after payment to wean the Russians into a debt settlement, the Russians attempted to use the debt as a means of getting closer collaboration from the Americans in the hope that they would want the payment badly enough to do something concrete to scare Japan, even if it were only a nonaggression pact.

When the Russians suggested a nonaggression pact in March of 1934, Bullitt contacted Washington to find out if the administration favored such an agreement. Bullitt was not enthusiastic about the proposal as he viewed it in the category of an entangling alliance. Hull informed his man in Moscow: "President's position with regard to a bilateral nonaggression pact is unchanged. He views with disfavor the idea of any nonaggression pact restricted to less than the whole group of Powers that have interests in the Pacific."[22] Although he had no intention of signing such a pact, Bullitt suggested in July that the discussions relative to the proposal should be used as a lever in reaching agreement on questions of debts and credits. Litvinov had heard that the Americans

124

were going to refuse to sign a pact and join the British in opposing Soviet admission to the London Naval Conference scheduled for 1935. Litvinov asked if these disturbing rumors were true, and Bullitt reported that he did not attempt to set the Russian's mind at ease. The American ambassador requested permission to string Litvinov along offering the prospect of closer collaboration in these matters if the Russians would live up to their obligations. In responding the Department of State did not suggest any other line of policy and recorded that a final decision had not been made on the pact.[23] In fact the decision had been made in March not to sign a pact. What had not been determined was whether to tell the Russians yet of the decision.

Bullitt wrote FDR and R. Walton Moore nearly identical letters on September 8 with the suggestion that a closer and more friendly relationship with the Japanese would bring the Russians scurrying to pay their debt and that was about the only thing that would change their minds, unless, of course, an attack by Japan again seemed imminent. As he did throughout his tenure as ambassador to Russia, Bullitt charged that Litvinov was the real block to an agreement. In his letter to Moore, Bullitt guessed that "His entire attitude is based on the belief that a real rapprochement between the United States and Japan is impossible. If he were to think for one minute that we might establish really good relations with Japan he would, of course, be scared to death. . . ."[24] The Russians were not so sure of American support as all that. What they were sure of was that there was as good a chance of war between the United States and Japan as between Russia and Japan, and if that eventuality occurred then cooperation in the Far East would be determined at a different level of understanding. In this context *Pravda* carried numerous articles in September, October, and November attempting to show that the rivalry between the U.S. and Japan had already gone to the edge of a hot war and that the struggle could not be far distant primarily due to Japanese attempts to limit American influence in the Far East which the Americans could not tolerate.

Given all the pluses which still appeared to be available through a genuine rapprochement in 1934 and given the desire for support in the international arena the Russians did not surrender their high hopes for cooperation and continued to grasp at every apparent gesture on the part of the Americans with renewed faith that it might lead to something. Thus when in 1934 the United States seemed to support the Litvinov Plan suggesting definitions of aggression and consultative pacts to be effective in case of aggression at the Geneva Disarmament Conference, Russian expectations regarding the fruits of rapprochement with the Americans were cautiously rising.

While the Russians were encouraged by the favorable American response to the Litvinov Plan, they were unaware that Hull was working fervidly against even mild support. FDR told the American representative to the disarmament conference, Norman Davis, that he favored the United States agreeing to consult; whereupon Hull argued that this would never be tolerated by public opinion. FDR backed down, and Davis was told to deny that the United States would agree in advance to any definite course of action in case of aggression. Despite the American reversal *Pravda* on July 3, 1934, announced to its readers that the United States was in full agreement with the Soviet Union concerning opposition to Nazi Germany.

By the end of 1934 the United States had not budged the Russians in the debt negotiations, and Bullitt and Hull decided to further pressure the Soviets. Early in 1935 Hull announced that debt negotiations with the USSR were being abandoned for the moment. Bullitt was on leave of absence at the time so the American chargé d'affaires informed Hull that Litvinov thought the American move to be a good idea. Negotiations could then be resumed, according to Litvinov, when the prospect for successful settlement was more opportune. Wiley, the chargé, asked Litvinov what inspired his optimism that there might be a better climate later. Litvinov replied that "political conditions would change and might greatly influence matters." Wiley judged that political conditions would not change all that much in the United States. Litvinov responded that he had conditions in Europe in mind. The chargé thought this a cryptic illusion. Wiley's perception was usually better than this, for it was obvious that Litvinov based his assessment on the assumption that the German menace would ultimately become so clear as to move the United States toward settlement on Russian terms.[25]

At this juncture the Soviets shifted their emphasis to an effort to gain British cooperation in isolating Germany. During a visit of Anthony Eden to Moscow Litvinov broached the subject of British efforts to publicly approve the Franco-Soviet arrangement against Germany which could make the Germans think twice regarding their aggressive plans for Europe. Eden seemed sympathetic but noncommittal. Nothing really came of the initiative.[26]

As the United States failed to move markedly in the direction of cooperation with the democratic states in 1935, they began to discount any role for the Americans. To a lesser degree this was also true in the USSR. President Roosevelt was fully aware of the European attitude towards the role of the U.S. in international relations. With reference to the USSR specifically and Europe generally he wrote to Bullitt:[27]

> I hope you are not being ostracized by the "information givers" at Moscow, though I gather that no European Capitol in the present confusion cares a continental damn what the United States thinks or does. They are very unwise in this attitude.

FDR assessed accurately the Soviet view of the declining importance of the United States at that particular juncture. This was shortly to be proved by a violation of the Litvinov pledge on propaganda at the Seventh Congress of the Communist International meeting in Moscow. Bullitt suspected that the pledge would be broken, but he was not sure of the degree to which the insults would be hurled. He proposed to the Department of State and the President several alternative responses to fit the severity of the violations ranging from a mild oral reprimand to the severance of relations. He cautioned that should the latter be the route the President took there would be severe ramifications.[28]

127

The results of a break in relations would, I think, be (1) Reduction of Soviet purchases in the United States; (2) A long period without relations since, if we break on the ground that the Soviet Government has not kept its pledges, it will be difficult for us later to say that we consider its pledges trustworthy; (3) The loss of an observation post in Moscow; (4) An increased chance that Japan will attack the Soviet Union; (5) A considerable decrease in the prestige of the Soviet Union and weakening of its present ascending influence.

In essence Bullitt advised that if the United States did not want any of these possibilities to become reality then she ought not to consider severance of relations as the route of protest.

When Bullitt decided to test the Soviet reaction to the possible disruption of relations, he did so at a party he gave at the American embassy. He told Karl Radek that he hoped the Comintern Congress would not result in so obvious a disruption of the Litvinov pledge as to force the United States to terminate diplomatic relations. Radek responded, "We have lived without the United States and we can continue to live without the United States. We shall never allow you to dictate to us what we may do or what we may not do in Moscow."[29] The degree to which the Soviet Union either did not care about the American reaction or did not expect the American government to carry through with Bullitt's threat was illustrated at the Congress where the United States was accused of moving rapidly toward a fascist system and mistreating the proletariat so badly that revolutionary activity there would soon be able to bear fruit. It was crucial, therefore, to create an anti-fascist party in the United States to which the workers could rally.[30] When the protest was delivered and relations were not severed the protest did not receive very much attention in the Soviet Press; however, the fulminations of the Comintern Congress against the United States did not receive much attention in the press either.

What did receive attention was an unusual interpretation of

the American neutrality legislation and the President's State of the Union message in 1936. On January 6 *Pravda* judged the message as deserving great attention because it showed "possible shifts in the position of the USA on many questions, of significance not only for the American continent but also for the entire world." In support of his contention the reporter indicated that FDR sharply criticized the policies of Japan, Germany, and Italy, but he warily noted that it was difficult to determine how far the United States would go to meet the efforts of states proposing collective security against the menacers of the peace. The Russians thought that while the usual American affirmation of neutrality was present the President spoke nonetheless to the real problems confronting peace loving states. Neutrality might, in other words, have a broad meaning. The new legislation seemed to the Russian observer to illustrate that the United States had "taken some steps toward cooperation with those European countries which support the collective [security] system."

Russian statesmen were willing at this stage to believe that the United States, recognizing the seriousness of an impending conflict, would join insofar as it could in guaranteeing the effectiveness of collective security efforts in Europe. That the Russians chose the neutrality legislation as an illustration of this willingness is more an illustration of the extent of their hopes than their ability to assess accurately what was happening in the United States. The last portion of the *Pravda* article is almost unbelievable given the actual intent of the framers of the neutrality legislation.

> Roosevelt's message testifies that there are in the USA influential circles which understand the significance of the principle of the indivisibility of the peace in the struggle against aggression and aggressors. This permits one to think that tendencies finding their expression in Roosevelt's message are not an accidental phenomenon. If the American government subsequently realizes even only what was noted in the presidential message, this could strengthen the front of the peaceful powers and become a deterrent to those countries who base

their policy on inciting a new world war.

This time it does not seem likely that the Soviets were trying to scare Germany with a strained interpretation of American neutrality because the realities of the situation would become obvious too soon. The Russians apparently believed that at last Roosevelt was coming forth with something that would do some good in support of insuring peace. FDR had spoken of the need to address himself to the serious crises arising on the international level and his determination that the United States should play the role of the "good neighbor," but the key sentence for the Russians was one on which they placed their own special interpretation. If they had uttered it they would mean forthcoming action to forestall an impending disaster. The President said,[31]

> Not only have peace and good-will among men grown more remote during this period, but a point has been reached where the people of the Americas must take cognizance of growing ill-will, of marked trends toward aggression, of increasing armament, of shortening tempers—a situation which has in it many of the elements that lead to the tragedy of general war.

Roosevelt, as the Russians understood him, had at that point in his address said that he recognized the aggressors for what they were and what they wanted, and he was going to stop them. Stopping them to the Russians meant collective security.

When shortly after this Key Pittman, Chairman of the Senate Foreign Relations Committee, said that it was time for Congress to be aware of Japan's policy in China and its influence on the United States because only Congress could grant the means to prepare for national defense, *Pravda* gave the speech full coverage in its February 12, 1935 issue. Congress seemed awake to the danger to peace also.

At this juncture the Russians now believed that they could play the carrot and stick game with the Americans for they were sure that the Americans and the Japanese were drifting

130

toward war. On February 17, Litvinov called Bullitt in for a discussion and informed him that Russia was now secure from an attack by Japan because the Japanese were convinced that they could not win unless Germany attacked at the same time. He felt that the prospect was not likely because their relationship to Germany had lately improved to the extent that the Germans were asking Russia to accept German credits in order to be able to buy German goods.[32]

Russia asked for action against Germany in the League in response to the German move into the Rhineland. At the same time Russian ambassadors in the various capitols of Europe and in the United States issued warnings that if Germany went unpunished for this the next step was general war; no one, no matter how much wishful thinking they might engage in, would be spared from participation. To all of this Bullitt reported to his friend R. Walton Moore that Russia was engaging in scare mongering. "The fundamental aim of the foreign policy of the Soviet Union," Bullitt reported, "is to keep Europe divided and the Soviet government can be counted on to do anything necessary to maintain a hearty hatred between France and Germany." There was indeed some truth in this, the main Russian fear was that everybody else in Europe and Asia was hoping to gain specifically at her expense. Not too many months after this letter Bullitt went home on leave and was quietly moved to a position as a consultant in the Department of State to Secretary Hull. No immediate plans were announced to replace him because, as the *New York Times* reported it, ". . .There are no pressing problems to render imperative the presence of an ambassador, as relations between Russia and the United States have been on a routine basis since the collapse of the debt negotiations."[34]

One of the most cogent expressions of the hopes and fears underlying Soviet foreign policy in this period was voiced by Litvinov to the Central Executive Committee of the Communist Party of the Soviet Union on November 10, 1936. *Izvestiia* recorded the address on the eleventh and explained that Litvinov warned that the aggressor nations were trying to convince other states that if they joined them in a crusade against the USSR all would profit. In reality, Litvinov argued, the aggressors wished to apply the old technique of divide and conquer. The Soviet Union, however, would continue to rely on her own means of defense having built up her war making power in order to become impregnable to attack. Having built such power the Russians could "wait quietly and see how Europe makes its choice. We know well that if other nations really want to organize peace, to guarantee collective security, and oppose to the forces of aggression the effective forces of peace, they cannot do it without the Soviet Union." The aggressors feared Soviet ability to organize the peace, Litvinov asserted, and as a result were attempting to isolate Russia from the West.

One lesson the Soviets learned from the high expectations they built in their citizens' minds when Bullitt was appointed ambassador was not to give the new appointee such a buildup. Thus when Joseph Davies' appointment was announced he got very slight play in the Russian press. On November 21, 1936, a two column seven line story appeared in *Izvestiia* stating that Davies had been appointed and what other government positions he had held. The *New York Times*, however, gave it a much larger play and foresaw significance in the appointment which could not fail to impress Russian officials who kept track of American newspaper opinion. The *Times* observed that the appointment not only killed some persistent rumors that FDR would leave the post vacant until the Russians settled their debts, but it illustrated the degree of importance which the President attached to Russian relations. Because of the Soviet connection to the Spanish revolution and the possible reactions to the agreement between Japan and Germany aimed at Russia, Roosevelt wanted the post filled quickly and with a person who could be counted on to further cordial relations between the United States and the USSR.[35]

If the Russians could have seen the final despatch Bullitt sent from Moscow before he left for home or the letter from George Messersmith, then serving in Austria, to R. Walton Moore which the latter forwarded to FDR, they would have had even higher hopes for future U.S. cooperation than they got from the *Times* article on Davies' appointment. Bullitt reported that although there were many things to try a man's soul in Russia they were traditional problems in Russia and not just communist ones. He predicted that the Soviet Union would play a great future role in the affairs of Europe and Asia. He felt relations must be maintained in order to know what was going on and to influence them as much as possible.[36] Messersmith argued the same line of reasoning which Litvinov used in his speech to the Central Executive Committee on November 10, except that Messersmith wrote his letter from Vienna on November 6. He charged that Germany was launching an offensive in Europe to isolate the Soviet Union from the West. Further, the Nazi charges that Russia was interfering in the internal affairs of other nations might have some truth in it, but such interferences were nowhere as pernicious and insistent as the same activities coming from Berlin. In essence Messersmith argued that while Russian interference was bad, Nazi interference was rotten and far more aggressively organized and directed.[37]

Pravda repeated an article which appeared in the Washington *Post* on December 1, 1936, which gave further credence to Soviet belief that the United States was not hopelessly lost to them as a partner in turning the screws for peace. The article in the *Post* stated that FDR was organizing the Latin American states to resist German and Japanese incursions into the Western hemisphere, but the *Pravda* writer chose to see this also as an illustration that Roosevelt was awakening to the threat of German and Japanese aggression and as a result was calling for collective action against the aggressors. Once again the Russians geared up for a possible rapprochement of some meaning with the Americans. The charge d'affaires at the American embassy in Moscow reported to the Department of State on January 15, 1937, that according to an official from the Foreign Office the Kremlin had issued orders to Litvinov that the irritations of the preceding three years were to be forgotten and "a new book in the relations between the Embassy and the Soviet Government is to be opened."[38] The ambassador himself wrote to Hull informing him that practically every Russian official from Washington to Moscow started their conversations by emphasizing the line—"let bygones be bygones" and "let's pick it up from here."[39] The Soviets gave some indication that just as Hull and Bullitt thought Litvinov was the block in getting the debt settled, they believed that Bullitt was the block to closer collaboration between the two powers in matters of mutual interest. The vituperation which the Russian press heaped on Bullitt as he left Moscow lends credence to this suspicion.

It took approximately until February for Litvinov to begin to test Davies on his perception of the dangerous situation in the world that they both had to be cognizant of and the degree to which there might now be cooperation to confront it. While the purge trials were going on and other embassies were being subjected to harassment and attacked in the press, the Americans were almost alone in being exempted from this sort of thing. Meanwhile Davies was assured over and over again that the United States was in a special category where foreign nations were concerned—neither feared nor hated. Davies was also given the softening up treatment via frequent visits to and from the foreign office and relatively free access to go where and when he pleased.

Then came a conversation with Litvinov which the ambassador passed on to Hull. In the course of a general discussion about the American position in the world Litvinov suggested that the United States was not so far removed from the world's troubles as she might believe and that world conditions were closing in on American isolationism especially where Japan was concerned. Davies responded that the U.S. was sufficiently remote from Japan and the Japanese sufficiently assured by American intentions as to be less dangerous than all that. For its calculated effect Litvinov turned his conversation to Europe and informed the American that Hitler was dominated by the ambitions expressed in *Mein Kampf*. His lust for conquest and for the domination of Europe meant that England had better look out because once Europe was gone he would "swallow the British Isles also."[40] The intent of this frank discourse was to both apprise Davies of the stakes of the diplomatic game in Europe and Asia and to get some impression of his concept of the situation. In the latter category Litvinov must have been disappointed because Davies did not let on that he was disturbed at all. Over the next two years, however, the ambassador's complacency

134

oozed away, and his reports on the danger emanating from Germany especially became less sanguine.

Like his predecessor Davies believed that his charm and persuasion along with the Russian desire for friendship could bring forth a debt settlement. Also like Bullitt he was to be disappointed, but unlike Bullitt Davies did not take it personally. When the debt question was brought up it was not by the American ambassador but rather through a group of Soviet officials including the People's Commissar for Foreign Trade, Rosengolts; People's Commissar for Defense, Marshall Voroshilov; the People's Commissar for Food Industries, Mikoyan; prosecutor in the Radek trial, Vyshinsky, and the new Amtorg representative, Rozov. Rosengolts invited Davies to his country Dacha where this impressive assemblage brought up the subject of the Russian debt.

Once again the Americans held out the carrot to the Soviets, but this time the subject was not broached by the Americans but by an influential group of Soviet leaders searching for some source of accommodation which they obviously felt to be necessary and warranted. Davies did not give specific promises of assistance, but he implied that the Russians would need American support in their coming struggle with their aggressive neighbors and that it could be forthcoming only after the debt question was settled.[41] In a letter to FDR Davies announced that he had handled the matter as they had discussed it before he left for the USSR.[42]

From the American embassy in Moscow the word came that the Russians were much concerned about the Nazi threat and that the intensity of press attacks on the Germans increased. The general tone of the report indicated that the Soviets were trying vigorously to draw all of their neighbors into some sort of a firm mutual assistance arrangement and to discredit, bully, or cajole those that were not inclined to see things the right way.[43]

Russian hopes relative to an active American policy of assistance were raised when Ambassador Davies decided to exert good offices in the dispute over Soviet-Japanese boundaries on the Amur River. Davies expressed his opinion to the Japanese Ambassador that the United States would be

135

happy to see the incident localized. Hull sent a sharp reprimand to the ambassador for acting without Departmental approval.[44] In other respects the Russians were led at this time to suspect an improved Soviet-American relationship aimed toward turning aside the aggressors. From the beginning of 1934 on the Russians attempted to get American naval vessels to visit a Soviet Far Eastern port in order to impress the Japanese with the developing cooperation between the two nations. On July 29, 1937, the long awaited visit was fully reported in *Pravda* as Admiral Harry Yarnell visited Vladivostok with American war vessels. According to *Pravda* this along with the hearty reception of Soviet airmen visiting the United States illustrated the growing rapprochement between the United States and the Soviet Union. Further evidence of this intent came from Troianovskii who wrote for *Pravda* on August 24 that the friendship then developing between the United States and the USSR "might easily become a foundation for the organization of the struggle for peace."

If the Russians believed this in August their hopes went soaring in October after FDR's Quarantine Speech delivered in Chicago, Illinois. The speech suggesting the quarantining of aggressors most specifically aimed at Japan was reprinted in full on the front pages of *Pravda* and *Izvestiia* on October 6. This was followed by reports from the United Press news agency that Washington diplomatic circles interpreted the address to be an open call for concrete action by peace loving nations with the goal of halting Japanese aggression in China. The same circles were also quoted as suggesting that the speech was a notification to the leading member nations of the League that the United States was ready for joint international action in defense of peace. The initiative, however, reportedly had to come from elsewhere before the U.S. would act. The Russians refrained from direct commentary on what the American action might be, but there were hints that *this time* action was expected.

For several weeks American statements on the international situation received front page coverage in the Russian press. The initiative was taken by other powers with American support in the calling of the Brussels Conference intended to deal with Far Eastern problems. Hopes were not raised too high, however, for Litvinov addressed the conference at its opening session with a warning of what was likely to happen if they did not take their charge directly to heart. Previously such conferences ran into trouble, he said, when they came into contact with the aggressors themselves and attempted to persuade them to alter their attitude. At the closing session of the Brussels Conference the fears expressed by Litvinov in the opening session were confirmed, and the Russian Vice Commissar for Foreign Affairs Vladimir Potemkin told the delegates as much: "...We are compelled to note with regret that all the efforts made by the Conference to terminate hostilities in the Far East by methods of mediation and conciliation have failed."[45] Potemkin concluded that this need not be true if some nation would take the lead in demanding that the existing treaties be upheld. Like the United States, however, Russia was not prepared to take the lead but would cooperate with those states who would take the initiative.

In an election address of November 27, Litvinov brought an old Soviet suspicion to the surface as to why "bourgeois" politicians who declared themselves to be against aggression did not act against the aggressors. He said that this audience might be puzzled regarding why experienced diplomats could fail to understand the meaning of the aggressors' tactics.[46]

> You think they are only pretending to disbelieve the aggressor's statements, and, under cover of negotiations for confirmation and explanations, they are groping for a deal with the aggressor. You can think so if you like, but my position does not allow me to express such doubts, and I must leave them to your responsibility. I can speak only about the official position of other States.

To some degree the Russians were confused about the American position. They decided that there was a struggle of some sort going on in the United States relative to the direction American foreign policy should take. They thought that there were some realistic elements in the American government structure trying to awaken the country to the threat of aggression and what it meant to American security. These forces were opposed by the isolationists and those who would like to see the aggressors settle all problems by wearing themselves out in a war with the Soviet Union. Many Russians thought that there was an anti-Soviet faction in the Department of State and said so. They were disturbed when Ambassador Joseph Davies was transferred to Belgium and there was no special effort to replace him with a new ambassador. But nevertheless a hopeful article appeared on page one of the January 1, 1938, issue of *Izvestiia* foretelling the growing strength of the anti-Japanese movement in the United States. *Pravda* referenced on January 4 the American awareness of Japanese espionage activity in the United States.

Like the Russian observers of the American scene many people in the United States assumed that they could see a new policy emerging. Letters poured in to the President, the Secretary of State, and individual Congressmen and Senators. Secretary Hull told a gathering of newsmen on March 17,[47]

> To waive rights and to permit interests to lapse in the face of their actual or threatened violation— and thereby to abandon obligations—in any important area of the world, can serve only to encourage disregard of any law and of the basic principles of international order, and thus contribute to the inevitable spread of international anarchy throughout the world.

Hull's address was noted prominently in *Izvestiia* on March 20 as indicating some new thoughts on foreign policy in the United States. The Russian paper asserted that Hull had made a major address to the National Press Club to explain American foreign policy, and in the process he had stated that the problems in the realm of foreign affairs had become questions of universal order or anarchy based on force. This view was dictated, the paper said, by the fact of the threat of large scale armed conflict in both Europe and Asia. Hull said, "We cannot, without subjecting ourselves to every danger, go any slower than in our presently proposed policy of armament." *Izvestiia* also told of Hull's desire to alter drastically the neutrality legislation and to "cooperate on the basis of common sense where mutual interests prevail" with other threatened nations, "always retaining, however, freedom of choice and action."

While the Russians liked to quote Hull on American awareness, real excitement was reserved for Roosevelt's ventures into the diplomatic realm, for they placed much more faith in his ability to move America in the right direction than anyone else. When FDR asked Congress for increased defense appropriations on January 4, *Pravda* became excited. On January 5 *Pravda* reported that informed circles in Washington expected the President in the near future to propose an additional program of military expansion in accordance with his message to Congress. The official circles, said the *Pravda* writer, emphasized the demand of the President for the augmentation of the Army to sufficient strength to put the United States in a position "to ensure a peaceful settlement of conflict." To the Russians it was especially significant that the President's concern was said by representatives of the State Department to include both Europe and Asia although it would not be so strong as to support treaty commitments.

FDR's move toward rearmament seemed to stir a belief in the Soviet Union that it was time to throw out some suggestions concerning possible rapprochement. At any rate the French Premier Léon Blum was told by the French ambassador to the USSR that Litvinov told him he had assured Norman Davis at the Brussels Conference that Russia would come to the aid of the United States if she were attacked by Japan. The American Ambassador to France William Bullitt forwarded the information to the Department on January 14 for confirmation.[48] Bullitt could not believe that Litvinov would say such a thing. He had apparently forgotten his own prediction in 1936 that the Soviets would profit from a victory over Japan by emerging in control of the Far East.[49] This was not the only statement concerning Soviet intent to participate in a general war in the Far East. The Chinese ambassador in Moscow repeatedly was told by Litvinov that the Soviet Union would declare war at once on Japan if England, France, and the United States did so. The ambassador, however, did not believe what he was told and insisted on knowing if Litvinov meant that Russia would fight if any of those powers entered a war with Japan or only if all three did so. Litvinov was evasive, he said.[50]

In response to Bullitt's query the Department informed him that Litvinov had asked at Brussels how far the United States was willing to go in coercive action. Davis told Litvinov that the United States was not considering coercive action at that time. Litvinov then indicated that "Russia would be quite prepared to act with England and the United States, but that she would want to feel certain that she would not be left the bag to hold." Hull told Bullitt that there was no mention of a war "even indirectly."[51] Apparently Secretary Hull and Litvinov differed in their interpretations of the nature of coercive action.

To *Izvestiia* President Roosevelt seemed to assume heroic proportions early in 1938, as the paper devoted an article to analyzing American foreign policy with the assistance of the American press. There was an intense campaign in the United States of the isolationists against the foreign policy of FDR. According to the Russian paper, there was a small group of Trotskyists who were actively supporting Japanese imperialism and denying that fascist aggression was a threat to the United States. The secretary of the "so-called Council for the Prevention of War," *Izvestiia* charged on February 14 was a supporter of fascism and a Japanophile who insisted on satisfying Germany and not cooperating with England.

Izvestiia played up the determination of Secretary Hull to make the issues clear in defense of American policy as the Secretary asserted, "cooperation is common sense. We must take into consideration the strength of other peace-loving nations and aim our strength to supplement theirs, as does every other country, or else the aggressors will be aided." Hull went on to qualify this apparent strong stand into meaningless rhetoric, but *Izvestiia* chose to ignore this.

Russia bent over backwards to convince the United States that they had a community of interests. Ambassador Troianovskii attempted to illustrate that Russia did not need the United States to defend her because she was adequately prepared for defense. At the same time he attempted to convince America that cooperation in defense of the peace was in her best interest. The Russian ambassador told the City Club in New York that his country was being placed on record as backing democratic nations, desiring continuance of their democratic forms of government, and urging "the democracies—including Russia, which he said has a government of Socialist-democracy and not communism—to present a united front against fascist peace breakers."[52] Troianovskii was obviously assigned the task of working on public and private opinion in the United States, since he delivered speech after speech pointing up the peril to security for everyone posed by the Nazi and Japanese menace.

Pravda relayed to its readers on June 22 the possibility of a forthcoming change in American policy as it repeated reports from Washington that Congress would review the whole problem of American foreign policy including the neutrality law. The writer stated, "The State Department intends in the near future to conduct a campaign, by mobilization of public opinion, in favor of the foreign policy of the government." The nature of the government's policy was presumably illustrated by President Roosevelt's attack on the "Fascist Barbarians" in a speech to the National Education Association on June 30. In reporting the speech on July 2, *Izvestiia* quoted FDR to the effect that several countries might attempt to turn back the progress of civilization, but the United States would act to preserve it. This imparted to the Russians the impression that the United States was ready to actively defend civilization.

V
America Is Moved to the Shelf

The Soviet dilemma concerning the direction of foreign policy was the indecision of the democratic nations to create a security front to meet the aggressors. Maxim Litvinov examined the problem before an election meeting in Leningrad and came out with a direct confrontation of the weaknesses which plagued statesmen of the democratic states in determining policy. He pointed out that the democracies were unprepared to face aggression. Litvinov desired that facts be faced. The Soviet Union had two choices because it had armed and announced a firm policy of resistance as soon as aggressive designs became obvious. Western states in failing to prepare were bereft of alternatives. Russia could cooperate with the Western nations in the preservation of peace or she could make deals with whomsoever would agree to deals and let the rest of the states fight it out. As Litvinov expressed it,[53]

> ...We know that, whatever deals the capitalist States may enter into among themselves, whatever combinations they may invent, the aggressors will always seek new prey in those territories whose masters have shown their flabbiness and their inability to defend their positions.

It remained unstated that in doing this aggressors would have to secure themselves from attack by the Soviets. Yet the threat of such a possibility was implicit. The time had come for the Western states to decide whether they feared the threat of communism by infiltration more than they feared the threat of fascism by force.[54]

Litvinov made it quite clear that the United States was in a special category. She felt no immediate threat and, therefore, could bear less responsibility for active leadership than European states to whom the threat was very close. "In the great trans-atlantic republic," Litvinov said, "isolationism has made such great headway that one can hardly reckon on its eventual cooperation, particularly if in Europe itself there is not formed beforehand a firmly welded group opposing aggression with an appreciable chance of success."[55]

This speech was a calculated warning that the time had really come, in FDR's terminology, "to fish or cut bait." After Munich when the Soviets considered themselves to be the object of British disaffection, the warning became even more explicit as Litvinov told the French ambassador that Russia would withdraw behind her frontiers, watching Germany grow fat on the rest of Europe. When the continent was subdued, whom would Hitler turn on, militarily prepared

142

Russia or weak foundering England? The answer, Litvinov thought, was England, and then she would have to beg for Soviet favors. In effect, he told the Frenchman that the Western democracies had helped to make Russia a power to be reckoned with.[5 6]

Litvinov's fears concerning the course of events were stated clearly to the Secretary of State in a despatch from Joseph Davies of April 1. He wrote that Litvinov was sure a fascist peace was being imposed on Europe. Russia could not count on outside aid and had to continue her own self-sufficiency, and France could not be depended upon at all. He believed that only a new government in England could save the day. Although the Secretary of State's pronouncement before the National Press Club on March 17 "was a great help," Litvinov said, "that without practical implementation it would, unfortunately, not be effective against the 'ruthless forces of fascism.' "[5 7]

Practical implementation of policy was of primary interest to the Soviets. They could not understand the repeated American protestations of the need for defending the peace and the refusal of American policy makers to follow up their intimation. Each time the Russians indicated that they might be losing faith in the possibility that America would ever make a cooperative effort against aggression Secretary Hull, the President, or some other member of the administration would make a speech implying forthcoming action or some other indication of a desire for collaboration in defending the peace.

Cooperative relations to the Soviets meant measures for collective security as Hull knew. Yet he had no real prospect of moving toward collective security with Russia. If he could not see his way clear to making an effective agreement with England, the one country which public sympathy favored, regarding the Far East, the area which was most likely to arouse public support for cooperation, he certainly would not risk rapprochement with the most unpopular country after Japan, Germany, and Italy. What purpose was there then in encouraging hope of cooperation? The answer lies, perhaps, in the statement of the embassy staff in Moscow in a composite report to the Secretary of State of November 25. The despatch noted that Munich had isolated the Soviets, and in lieu of European allies they sought even closer ties with the United States as the writers believed was indicated in an article which they referred to entitled "The Two Giants," by Alex Sandrov, which had appeared in *Izvestiia* and one from *Krasnaia-Zvesda* entitled "Soviet-American Relations."

Under the circumstances the embassy personnel thought the United States had the Soviets in a position to take advantage of their eagerness in order "to bring about a profitable settlement of outstanding matters of which the solution has been delayed owing to difficulties either actual or assumed which the Soviet Government had adduced in the course of past negotiations."[58] This reference, of course, was primarily to debts and propaganda, which reflected the basic concern of the Department of State and the disinclination to take seriously the prospect of real cooperation with the Soviets in the interest of security. The embassy staff understood that Secretary Hull considered cooperation as constituting "genuine friendship." They notified the Secretary that it should be noted that no statement could be found in the articles that they thought indicated a real desire for friendship, as Hull understood it, on the part of the Kremlin. The despatch concluded, "It may be assumed that the Kremlin does not envisage cordial relations with the capitalist governments on any permanent basis but rather as a temporary expedient dictated by the more immediate objectives of Soviet policy."[59]

One of the articles referred to in the embassy despatch illustrated indeed a most friendly disposition toward the United States. The Soviets made no effort to hide their conviction that their concept of friendship was based on mutual self-interest and expediency. The problem which plagued Soviet-American relations was that the Russians thought that the Americans understood the basis of Soviet policy and considered their needs and American needs regarding security to be similar enough to make cooperation a reality. "The Munich policy," Sandrov wrote in the November 16 *Izvestiia* article,

...has placed new problems before even the most

144

powerful capitalist state which took no part in the Munich agreement, namely the United States of America. The leaders of American policy...have long been aware of the real significance of events in question [in Europe and Asia] and are able to evaluate and characterize with calmness and strength the state of affairs which has arisen.

Thus having visualized a group of realists in charge of manipulating American policy, it was not difficult for Sandrov to imagine that even before the crises of September, FDR, Hull, Welles, Secretary of the Interior Harold Ickes, and others who opposed the "lying campaign of the isolationists" had indicated clearly that they knew peace was indivisible and the security of the United States depended on the security of other states. The various pronouncements of the members of the administration were taken as something other than name calling, and the Russians anticipated that they might lead to a genuine break in tradition. The United States, Sandrov analyzed, could in no way remain indifferent in the face of outright violations of her interests, especially from Japan, and American statesmen "often proclaimed the necessity of collective action in repelling aggression." If the Russians understood that this meant collective moral action, they did not indicate it. That no collective action was forthcoming was explained on the basis of the failure to implement the Quarantine Speech because of internal political problems and especially because of the attitude of Great Britain.

By the time this article appeared the Soviets had gone into virtual isolation. They had abandoned much hope of getting any effective assistance from France, and it seemed obvious to them that England was trying desperately to salvage peace at Russia's expense. Russia then turned in a last effort toward rapprochement with the United States, the one nation with which she believed she had the most in common and the least possibility of imminent conflict. Sandrov pointed out, in fact, that the two nations had similar vital interests which were threatened by aggressors in both Europe and the Far East, and he felt the time had come when the United States had to choose a course for her future foreign policy. "Both countries," Sandrov concluded,

> can yet meet [on the road to the active defense of
> peace] and that would have the most salutary
> influence on the international situation. At this time
> we should remember the words of Litvinov in his
> speech at the banquet in New York on November
> 24, 1933, "who can doubt but that the united
> voices of the two giants will compel themselves to
> be taken into consideration, and that their joint
> efforts will weigh the scales to the benefit of
> peace."

The two giants, however, were separated by a wide gulf.
The United States imagined that in part her isolation from
Russia was ideological. The Soviets imagined that it was more
likely fear of public opinion in America, and this they found
hard to comprehend. They felt that if the administration
really desired to, it could seize the leadership of public
opinion and turn it in the direction of collective action. When
it appeared that this was occurring via speeches of Ickes and
others who sounded an alarm against Germany, they assumed
that a new cooperative policy would follow. The President
added to this belief himself with his speeches and press
announcements on the threat to America through South
America, and this too came to the attention of the Russians.
It was noted in an *Izvestiia* article of December 4 that the
United States was cognizant of the existence of a serious
threat and knew what to do about it. *Izvestiia* speculated that
the solution of the problem lay in United States cooperation
with the countries of Europe and Asia who were interested in
preserving peace and repulsing aggressors.

What the Russians did not know was that the United
States had no policy but merely an attitude. She felt a threat
and at first recoiled. When the threat did not dissolve,
President Roosevelt rushed forward to do verbal battle
without being sure of the locus of the battlefield or the exact
nature of the weapons. Both giants felt themselves to be
isolated, but by the end of 1938 there was, perhaps, more
justification for this feeling in Russia than the United States.

In later years Soviet historians looked back on the events of 1938 searching for some foundations for American policy and concluded, like many American revisionists, that the government could not have been so incredibly blind to American interests. They felt that there was, therefore, some Machiavellian master plot aimed at embroiling Russia in a destructive war with Germany. Only after the failure of this policy did the United States attempt a rapprochement with Russia to defeat the Nazis. The Russians could not believe the truth.[60]

If 1938 proved the high point of Soviet expectations for cooperation with the United States in mutual security matters after recognition, 1939 saw the rapid decline of such beliefs. The year opened with another appeal to Congress by President Roosevelt for increased armaments and an implied warning. "We have learned," said FDR,[61]

> that God-fearing democracies of the world which observe the sanctity of treaties and good faith in their dealings with other nations cannot forever let pass, without effective protest, acts of aggression against sister nations—acts which automatically undermine all of us.

FDR's statement would not be challenged by any of the threatened governments, except perhaps the Soviet Union which would have taken mild offense at the use of the term God-fearing. There was, however, a wide variance of opinions on what constituted effective protest. Neville Chamberlain thought it meant American willingness to follow England's lead, though he did not expect for one moment that such a thing would happen. French government officials would have been satisfied with a declaration that America had vital interest in maintaining the European status quo and would defend those interests. They were slightly more hopeful of this prospect than the English or perhaps more desperately desired to believe in an aroused America. The Russians would have welcomed the sort of action requested by the French but hoped with less realism than the French for something more concrete than a declaration. The Russians hoped for an

147

alliance incorporating the principle of collective security for the Far East if not elsewhere. It is perhaps a remarkable commentary on the firm belief of the Russians that no nation could ignore its vital interests that they still felt that President Roosevelt meant the same thing that they did when he spoke of effective protests.

In examining the President's message the initial observations in Russia were cautious as *Izvestiia* on January 5, 1939, declared that Roosevelt asked Congress to review the neutrality law and to increase American armament so that an aggressor could be repulsed if necessary. It was also announced that the United States foresaw the eventuality of attack and hoped to avoid measures which might encourage or aid it. There was in this article no hint of great enthusiasm over what the President had said. However, after the American press had vociferously proclaimed FDR's message as an indication of a great departure in foreign relations, the Russians quoted American newspapers liberally.

On January 6 *Izvestiia* presented the view of the American press that it considered the address to be a "definite warning to the fascist aggressors," noting also that there was a distinct threat of applying economic sanctions. The English and French press were also liberally quoted by way of illustrating the new Roosevelt policy.

One of President Roosevelt's real problems in 1939 lay in the attempts of the administration to make drastic alterations of or to eliminate completely the existing neutrality law. It was a test of executive authority in the control of foreign affairs which was very carefully watched from abroad and especially from the Soviet Union. When the President told a peace conference on March 7 the war referendum concept was a serious threat to American security and the neutrality laws had injured the cause of world peace, his remarks appeared in *Izvestiia* two days later.

Pravda and *Izvestiia* followed the struggle for neutrality revision closely over the next few months. On July 21 *Izvestiia* took note of the fact that the struggle was over, and Roosevelt had lost. Hull and Roosevelt, the paper said, had staked their case on the basis of the argument that the danger of war in Europe was imminent. They wanted a review of the

148

neutrality law in order that the United States might have more influence on the outcome of events. Despite this strong appeal, the paper reported, Senator Borah refused to budge, and the Democrats had to concede that it would be impossible for the President to swing a majority. Late in the night, the Russian paper concluded, the President and the Secretary of State announced that they still felt that failure to review the neutrality law had weakened the United States' position in international affairs. The Russians soon were to give evidence that they agreed.

Before the Soviets gave up on the United States and the allies generally in 1939 there was one last surge of hope which rested on what the Soviets visualized as a changed relationship between the United States and Russia's ally France. On February 2 *Izvestiia* said that President Roosevelt had been closeted with members of the Senate Military Affairs Committee which was in charge of an inquiry into the facts connected with the sale of war planes to the French. During the last week of January a United States military plane carrying a Frenchman crashed with secret equipment aboard. This brought forth charges from the Hearst press that a secret military alliance existed between the United States and France. At a press conference the President explained the presence of the Frenchman as a result of a legitimate sale of aircraft authorized by the government.[62] President Roosevelt, the Russian press observed, denied the charge that the United States gave France important aviation secrets but noted that despite the fact that the President's deliberations with the Senate Military Affairs Committee were secret, well-informed correspondents were able to report a few details. According to reports from the Washington correspondents of the *New York Times*, the *Herald Tribune*, and others, *Izvestiia* noted:

Roosevelt declared to the members of the committee that France appears to be the first line of defense of the USA and that the US will give help to France and England against Germany. As they report it, Roosevelt, defending the sale of war planes to France, declared that the US must sell arms to England and France for strengthening the

149

democratic countries against the "Rome-Berlin-Tokyo" Axis.

Russian observers noted two significant aftereffects of this incident. *Izvestiia* said on February 3 that the fascist press "displayed skepticism and equinimity" concerning this presumed effort at aiding France. The Germans, *Izvestiia* observed, sneered that Roosevelt was "another Wilson." Obviously the fascist powers did not really believe that the United States was going to do anything effective. Two days later *Izvestiia* relayed FDR's vehement denial that he had said that the United States' defensive borders were in France. FDR assured the nation that the United States was not allied to anyone and that her policy had not changed in the slightest.

What happened in the United States bore a direct relationship to what the evolution of Russian policy was to be. The Russians were genuinely concerned lest British efforts at Munich and after might be directed toward turning the Germans against the Ukraine, and the United States was fully aware of this fear of Russia as it was reported to the Department of State several times from the embassy in Moscow and elsewhere. Alexander Kirk, the chargé of the American embassy in Moscow, reported that the Soviet Union was feeling the pulse of both sides to ascertain the signs of the most life, for at that stage of developments "whatever its attitude or aims may be, any positive move by the Kremlin in foreign affairs will, it is believed, depend on the development of events abroad."[63]

Kirk's prediction rang true, and the development of events abroad were boding ill for further success in the field of collective security. America, however, still remained the unknown quantity. Roosevelt, according to *Izvestiia* articles on February 20 and 23, was fighting for recognition of the threat to American security and rushing to build an effective defense mechanism, but the prospects for success were much in doubt.

On the American side of developments it became more and more obvious to the Department of State observers on the scene that events could go either way as far as the Russians were concerned. Kirk notified Hull on February 22 that

150

rumors were afloat in Moscow that Maxim Litvinov might be removed as Commissar of Foreign Affairs and assigned to replace Troianovskii as ambassador to the United States. In Kirk's opinion, if such a thing occurred, it would seem likely that collective security which had been championed by Litvinov had been abandoned in favor of a policy of rapprochement with Nazi Germany, to which Litvinov had always been strongly opposed.[64]

Shortly after this communication it was decided to appoint another ambassador to replace Davies who had left Russia in May, 1938. The new man was Laurence A. Steinhardt whose appointment was announced on March 5. Despite the information concerning the critical nature of events developing in Moscow, Steinhardt was told that he need not report to Russia until early August. The delay was one more illustration to the Russians that the Americans were not particularly eager to work out any rapprochement with them.

From the point of view of Soviet-American relations two very important events were recorded in the Russian press on March 10 and 11. On the tenth *Izvestiia* related that the former Secretary of State of the United States Henry L. Stimson, in a letter to the *New York Times*, asked that the United States stand with other powers against aggressive fascists who threatened the security of the United States as well. The Russian paper quoted Stimson's request for the United States to support "clearly" the Western powers in opposing the aggressors, and they would not dare carry the war any further. "Clearly" was the key word, for the Russians had reached the point where they felt that positive agreements had to be made with one side or the other, and there were groups which favored each side in the struggle between the democracies and the fascist oriented states. Since both were essentially enemies of the Soviet system and vice versa, the course of Soviet policy would be dictated purely by what the Kremlin considered to represent Russia's best interests.

The second important event was a speech by Stalin delivered to the Eighteenth Party Congress on March 10. Stalin's speech was forwarded to the Department of State on March 11 by Kirk. The charge' recorded that Stalin charged the democratic states with capitulation to the aggressors in order to preserve the fascist wall which stood between Russia and the West in the vain hope that fascist attentions would turn eastward rather than westward. The United States was connected by mention of the instigations of the North American press which spread "false stories" about Russian military weakness and other such comments in the hope of convincing the Germans that Russia would be an easy victim. This marked Stalin's first anti-American comments in some time and illustrated that the man at the top was getting ready to abandon Litvinov's appeal for collective security. In the concluding section of the address, however, Stalin also made a pitch to Germany as he noted that his task was to cement relations with all countries and to deal with whichever states were willing to respect Russia's integrity.

That Stalin was aiming at rapprochement with Germany is beyond question. Molotov said as much on August 23, after the Nazi-Soviet Pact was concluded. On that occasion Molotov toasted Stalin who "through his speech of March of this year, which had been well understood in Germany—had brought about the reversal in political relations."[65] Indeed the speech was followed by a whole series of exchanges between Russians and Germans at various contact levels. The process was analyzed accurately by a number of Americans in Europe. Kirk informed Hull of such a prospect on April 7, and he warned that if Litvinov went out as Foreign Affairs Commissar rapprochement with Germany could soon follow. Litvinov tried desperately to work out some agreement with the British and French in 1939, for he knew what the alternative was. Stalin gave him until May. Then he took over, and the door closed on collective security for all practical purposes. Litvinov was replaced after his forced resignation on May 3 by Molotov who leaned in the direction of the German rapprochement, and the issue was nearly settled. If the United States, Great Britain, or France came through in the early summer with positive commitments to Russian security, there could have been a turnabout, but Litvinov's replacement implied Stalin's belief that no such switch would take place.

In the same manner that the Soviet press set forth the message for the Germans, on June 7 *Pravda* gave the terms for a rapprochement to England and France. Molotov, *Pravda* said, presented for the English and French the minimum conditions necessary to establish a "united peace front." A pact of mutual aid among the countries concerned was essential with England and France agreeing to guarantee the Baltic countries, with concrete commitments on the methods, form and size of aid. The USSR, it said, could not guarantee the security of the countries tied to England, such as Poland, without reciprocity, which implied the need of recognizing which countries were tied to Russia.

Pravda stated the terms for cooperation by quoting a French newspaper. The French paper noted that England and France had to ask themselves the question, "Do we or do we not want a union with the USSR?" If this were desirable then it stood to reason that England and France had to put the USSR in a stronger diplomatic position than the one she occupied and prevent her being attacked through the Baltic states. Of course, if they did not want an alliance then the Baltic nations would have to be sacrificed to the Germans and "the Soviet Union does not want this and neither do we." Stripped of its niceties this was a blunt demand for Russian hegemony over the Baltic region as part of the expense of posing a hostile threat to Germany and of keeping Poland independent. The latter nation was mentioned by saying it would be nice to see her free, but who could tell what would happen if Russia had to worry about her frontiers on the Baltic. England and France did not feel that they could or should give Russia the guarantees she desired. Germany was only too willing to do so, and the die was cast.

By this time the United States was reduced to the role of interested observer. The Russians gave up on her and in fact turned to contemptuous comments about American objection to the development of events in Europe. The Russian press carried a series of articles on the Americans which were insulting and suggested that the United States should mind her own business, but even these were not as vituperative as those directed toward England and France. Hull told Steinhardt to suggest that a lenient attitude on the part of Russia toward Finland would help to soothe rising public passions against the Soviet Union in the United States.

Russia had passed beyond the stage where she felt that she could be primarily concerned about American public opinion or that she needed to be. She had already, by virtue of her agreement with Germany, absorbed, for all practical purposes, Estonia and Lithuania, and Germany had made it clear to Finland that she could expect no help from the Germans against Russia. The German Foreign Office informed its minister to Finland on October 9 that it did not believe that Russia would ask much of Finland, but if she did it was a matter to be settled between Russia and Finland.

Stalin, of course, had been the master plotter behind the entire maneuver from the first feeler after Munich to the thrust at Finland. He had never been comfortable in the company of the Western democracies, for generally they did not speak the same language of statecraft that he did. He gave Litvinov, however, the better part of a decade to persuade the democratic states to make agreements concerning commercial and defensive measures. Litvinov's dominance as Foreign Commissar depended on the success of rapprochement with England, France, and the United States. Failure of this policy was sure to see his decline and even his possible elimination. When the dismissal of Litvinov occurred, it should have received more careful attention from the democratic states than it did.

Russia warned repeatedly that failure of collective security would lead to other and more drastic measures. The preservation of Russian security and the vacillation and half-hearted policy of England and France had, as the Soviets said themselves, put Russia in the driver's seat where she could sell her wares to the highest bidder. France made her bids in the pacts with Russia of 1935 and after. They were useless, however, without complementary agreements with England in Europe or between the United States and Russia in Asia, for Germany had to be threatened effectively from one direction or the other. Russia could not help France in blocking German advances with an unchecked Japan roving her Siberian frontiers. The failure to make realistic bids to the Russians then must be laid at the feet of England and the United States, for France had little choice but to follow England's lead. But primarily England must bear the brunt of the responsibility for the failure of European security measures. The term responsibility is used cautiously to intimate that the action carried with it *some* indication of opprobrium, which it did. Neville Chamberlain took a highly calculated risk in hoping that Hitler's appetite was whetted for a large slice of Slavdom, and in doing this he gambled against extremely high odds that the Germans would attack their strongest potential enemy first.

If Chamberlain failed to wear the totalitarians down in internecine warfare, a simple calculation of alternatives should have indicated the probability that Russia would play turn-about. England, unprepared as she was for conflict, was in a poor position to play the armed powers off against one another without some sort of commitment to one of them, and Russia was the only one which was determinedly against an extension of the war at that time. Here also FDR failed to understand the alternatives.

In the final analysis, however, it was not President Roosevelt's failure to enter into effective agreements with the Russians for securing the peace in the 1930's which gave cause for criticism of the conduct of American foreign affairs, for such an alliance would have been good only so long as the Russians found it of special aid in the preservation of their own security. Criticism is justified because the Roosevelt administration followed a policy of drift in foreign affairs until the United States found herself in the position of being forced to choose between the lesser of two evils among the totalitarian states if democracy was to survive it all. American aid might not have helped. England and France might not have responded to a more direct policy of leadership from the United States, but the results of the attempt could scarcely have been more injurious than the policy of inaction which evolved. As Roosevelt waited for a policy, Stalin prepared to abandon Litvinov's plan for rapprochement with the West and to rekindle in the Russian heart old dreams of empire. While the German *drang nach Osten* had not yet run its course, the Russian drive to the West had already begun.

[1] In a previous study the author has examined this subject more exhaustively than it will be treated here. For further information see: Edward M. Bennett. *Recognition of Russia: An American Foreign Policy Dilemma* (Waltham, MA: Ginn/Blaisdell Publishing Co., 1970), pp. 139-150. Cited hereafter as Bennett, *Recognition of Russia*.

[2] Vladimir I. Lenin, *The Collected Works of V. I. Lenin* (New York: International Publishers, 1929), IV, 114.

[3] Joseph V. Stalin, *The Collected Works of J. V. Stalin* (Moscow: Foreign Language Publishing House, 1953), V, 206.

[4] Michael Cherniavsky, "The History of the Soviet Opinion of the United States, 1936-1946, As Expressed in Russian Newspapers, Journals, Books and Other Sources" (unpublished M.A. thesis, Dept. of History, University of California, 1946).

[5] Paul V. Harper (ed.), *The Russia I Believe In: The Memoirs of Samuel N. Harper, 1902-1941* (Chicago: University of Chicago Press, 1945), p. 249.

[6] Articles from *Izvestiia, Pravda*, and other Russian periodicals will not be footnoted, but dates and the names of the papers will be given in the text.

[7] Bullitt to FDR, January 24, 1933; Bullitt to FDR, January 26, 1933, Franklin Delano Roosevelt Library, Hyde Park, N.Y. Cited hereafter as FDRL, President's Personal File, 1124, William C. Bullitt Folder.

[8] Jane Degras (ed.), *Soviet Documents on Foreign Policy, 1933-1941* (London: Oxford University Press, 1953), III, 5. Cited hereafter as Degras, *Soviet Documents*, III.

[9] FDRL, The Henry Morgenthau, Jr. Papers, the Morgenthau Diaries— Farm Credit Diary, April 1933, p. 21.

[10] *Ibid.*, May 22, 1933, p. 31.

[11] For details of Roosevelt's investigation see Bennett, *Recognition of Russia*, pp. 87-112.

[12] Charge d'affaires ad interim Riga, Latvia to Secretary of State, October 27, 1933, U.S. Department of State Files 711.61/319 (National Archives, Washington, D.C.). Cited herafter as DSF.

[13] Memorandum, Hornbeck to Phillips, October 31, 1933 and Hornbeck to Hull, October 28, 1933, DSF 711.61/33.

[14] Degras, *Soviet Documents*, III, 452.

[15] *Ibid.*, 43.

[16] Bullitt to Secretary of State and President, December 24, 1933, FDRL, President's Secretary's File, Box 15. Cited hereafter as PSF.

[17] Andre de Laboulaye to Paul-Boncour, 21 Novembre 1933, Documents Diplomatiques Francais, 1932-1935, Vol. V (13 Novembre

1933-13 Mars 1934), Doc. 37, 64-65.

[18]Louis Fischer, "Behind Russian Recognition," *Nation*, CXXXVIII (January, 1934), 9-10.

[19]Degras, *Soviet Documents*, III, 71.

[20]Louis Fischer, "Litvinov's Diplomatic Year," *Fortnightly*, CXLI (February, 1934), 129-134.

[21]Bullitt to R. Walton Moore, March 19, 1934, FDRL, the R. Walton Moore Paper, Cited hereafter as Moore Papers.

[22]Hull to Bullitt, March 17, 1934, DSF 711.6112 (Aggressor)/2.

[23]Hull to Bullitt, July 10, 1934, DSF, 711.6112 (Aggressor)/9.

[24]Bullitt to FDR, September 8, 1934, PSF Russia, 1934; Bullitt to Moore, September 8, 1934, Moore Papers.

[25]Wiley to Hull, February 5, 1935, PSF Russia.

[26]"Digest of Important Developments in Foreign Affairs," April 2, 1935, PSF Russia.

[27]FDR to Bullitt, April 21, 1935, PSF Russia.

[28]Bullitt to Moore, July 15, 1935, Moore Papers.

[29]*Ibid.*

[30]Seventh World Congress of the Communist International, Dimitroff-Working Class Unity—Bulwark Against Fascism, Communist International Publications Resulting from Various Congresses. University of Illinois Library, Radical Pamphlet Collection.

[31]Samuel I. Rosenman (ed.), *The Public Papers and Addresses of Franklin D. Roosevelt* (New York: Random House, 1938), V, 89-92.

[32]Bullitt to Department of State, February 17, 1936, DSF 711.61/594.

[33]Bullitt to Moore, March 30, 1936, Moore Papers.

[34]"Bullitt Takes Post as Hull 'Consultant': Ambassador Denies Political Activity," *New York Times*, August 5, 1936, p. 13.

[35]"J. E. Davies Named as Our Ambassador to the Soviet Union," *New York Times*, November 21, 1936, p. 1.

[36]U.S. Department of State, *Foreign Relations of the United States, Diplomatic Papers: The Soviet Union, 1933-1939* (Washington: Government Printing Office, 1952), pp. 389-396. Cited hereafter as *FRUS: Soviet Union*.

[37]R. Walton Moore to FDR, November 27, 1936 (Enclosure: Letter from Messersmith to Moore of November 6, 1933), PSF II Departmental Files, Box 24.

[38]Henderson to Department of State, January 15, 1932, DSF 123 Davies, Joseph E./37.

[39]Davies to Hull, January 19, 1937, DSF 123 Davies, Joseph E./38.

[40]Davies to Hull, February 6, 1937, DSF 123 Davies, Joseph E./44.

[41]*FRUS, The Soviet Union*, p. 371.

[42]Davies to FDR, February 17, 1937, PSF.

[43] Henderson to Hull, April 27, 1937, DSF 761.00/284.

[44] Davies to Hull, July 1, 1937; Hull to Davies, July 2, 1937; DSF 761.9415 Amur River/17 and DSF 761.9415 Amur River/17A.

[45] Degras, *Soviet Documents*, III, 265.

[46] *Ibid.*

[47] U.S. Department of State, *Peace and War: United States Foreign Policy, 1931-1941* (Washington: Government Printing Office, 1943), p. 411.

[48] U.S. Department of State, *Foreign Relations of the United States, 1938* (Washington: Government Printing Office, 1955), III, 22. Cited hereafter as *FRUS*, 1938.

[49] *FRUS: The Soviet Union*, p. 294.

[50] *FRUS*, 1938, III, 19-20.

[51] *Ibid.*, 25, 26.

[52] *New York Times*, February 27, 1938, p. 1.

[53] Degras, *Soviet Documents*, III, 293.

[54] *Ibid.*, 292.

[55] *Ibid.*, 290.

[56] Robert Coulandre, *De Stalin a Hitler* (Paris: Hachette, 1950), p. 171.

[57] *FRUS: The Soviet Union*, p. 544.

[58] *Ibid.*, p. 593.

[59] *Ibid.*, pp. 593-594.

[60] This thesis is fully developed in the Soviet historical journal. See U. V. Arrotunian, "The Role of American Diplomacy in the Organization of the Munich Conference," *Voprosi Istorii*, No. 2 (February, 1958), pp. 76-95.

[61] Samuel I. Rosenman (ed.), *The Public Papers and Addresses of Franklin D. Roosevelt* (New York: Random House, 1939), VI, 3.

[62] Press Conferences of Franklin D. Roosevelt, XIV, No. 522, January 31, 1939, p. 102 ff. FDRL.

[63] *FRUS: The Soviet Union*, p. 732.

[64] *Ibid.*, p. 737.

[65] Memorandum of a Conversation Held on the Night of August 23rd to 24th, Between the Reich Foreign Minister, on the One hand, and Herr Stalin and the Chairman of the Council of People's Commissars Molotov, on the Other Hand. Raymond James Sontag and James Stuart Beddie, (eds.) *Nazi-Soviet Relations, 1939-1941: Documents from the Archives of the German Foreign Office*, Department of State, Washington, D.C., 1948, p. 76.

PERSPECTIVE

Professors Payne and Callahan have set forth conclusions in their essays so strikingly similar to those to which my research led me that a commentary on their perspectives becomes relatively easy; it requires assessment of only a few differences of viewpoint. By focusing on Russian, British, and French expectations regarding American assistance without prior consultation, it is apparent that we found largely the same concerns among the leaders of the three governments. That the British expected less than the others from the Americans was due in part to their better understanding of American politics and to their lower estimate of American ability to evaluate realistically threats to the security of the United States until the danger was real and present.

Relative power positions in the nineteen-thirties left three of the European allies of World War I in desperate straits as they confronted the nations attempting to upset the balance of power and seek preeminent positions in the world. For the first time in centuries England, France, and Russia found themselves simultaneously weakened economically, politically, and militarily in the face of a rising combination of nations wishing not merely to supplant them in the Great Power structure but to conquer and strip them of every semblance of such power. To some degree, each of the former allies sought reassurance from the others that they understood threats to security and national interests to be the same for all of them while not believing that the others could see their dependent positions with the same clarity. Instead of cooperation in the name of collective security, mutual suspicions led to recriminations and to desperate scrambling for assurances that they would not be left alone to confront the aggressively inclined powers; in the case of England and Russia this led to attempts to turn aside the aggressors by appeasement with the hope that Germany would turn her efforts against one of the others. This is not to say that Neville Chamberlain went to Munich primarily with the idea of freeing England from any possible danger by turning the Nazis eastward; rather it is to note as suggested in Roger

Bjerk's excellent dissertation study of Joseph Kennedy's ambassadorial career that Kennedy and Chamberlain both foresaw such a *possibility* and believed that when Hitler next moved it might *not* be westward. Chamberlain indeed hoped that there would be no war at all or if there should be one that England might be better prepared for it than at the time of Munich. France, as the power in the middle, tried desperately to reach agreements with the other former allies. She alone had not thought of appeasement for she felt that Germany could not be accommodated without losses to her which were inadmissible.

Failing to reach satisfactory arrangements and bereft of alternatives because of their isolation from one another and weakness in the face of the armed and aggressive forces of Germany, Italy, and Japan, France and Russia searched for a third force not directly competing with them to exert pressure on their enemies. They placed their reliance on the United States to confront the dissident nations because she had emerged as the most powerful state in terms of wealth and resources after the World War and seemed least likely to seek territorial expansion. Also, as the largest creditor to all three powers as well as equally threatened by restrictive trade practices in Europe and the Far East, she seemed bound more closely to them.

British statesmen were less inclined to seek American aid because they were strongly convinced that the Americans were likely to offer nothing but advice. This does not mean that the British gave up on the Americans altogether. In fact they did seek American commitments and cooperation in the Far East where they saw mutual interests as most inextricably bound to face Japanese incursions on trade and territorial possessions. Britain could no longer afford to police the world with a fleet that was dwindling in size relative to the tasks of defense and so the Americans had to take up the slack. The United States did not have direct territorial interests to protect in Europe, but she did have Hawaii, American Samoa, and the Philippines to worry about in the Pacific. This led British statesmen to believe that in those environs the Americans might take the lead in braking Japanese expansion. Thus in this area at least British and Russian diplomats

160

expected the same thing from the United States.

Professor Payne's contribution is replete with references to French expectations of American action during the decade and the hopes of French diplomats and statesmen that the United States must recognize mutuality of interests and come to France's aid because their enemies and obligations were so intertwined. In addition to the obvious accumulation of the sinews of power the French thought the United States could be called upon because of the American reputation for supporting "just" causes, that is, upholding treaty obligations. If France could get the Americans to sign a treaty more binding than the Pact of Paris, they would be tied to the French security system. The Russians held similar views concerning the Americans.

Also, like the Russians, French hopes were bound to rise when any American official expressed sympathy with their plight. This accounts for the grasping at straws such as French gratitude for inclusion in the Washington Treaties, hopes beyond reason for the closer ties which were, in the French view of it, implied in the Pact of Paris, and in the expectations of the Stimson cult, the Roosevelt cult and the Bullitt cult. Payne makes it clear that the French statesmen engaged in much self-deception, wishful thinking about overcoming isolationism, and excessive hopes concerning their ability to educate Americans to their similarity of interests because they thought themselves to be dependent upon such an awakening. The French sought American heroes and villains to account for their high hopes and the failure of those expectations.

Britain too played the role of villain for the French, and the Russians suspected the Anglo-Saxon combination and blamed the British for not attempting to overcome American isolationism and for not convincing their American cousins of the need for collective security. Fear, suspicion, and timidity affected British, French, Russian and American statesmen. They all expected someone else to take the leading role opposing aggression, and they would follow at their own pace. The Russians were able to do more in their own defense, but were *most* suspicious of others' motives among a group all of whom were suspicious.

161

Public opinion played a significant role in holding back effective cooperation in the United States, Great Britain, and France while in Russia the stumbling block was the antagonism of the old Bolsheviks to *any* cooperation with capitalist states. Americans generally disliked the Soviet system and held its leaders in contempt, but Francophobia and Anglophobia were more constant and bitter because citizens and governments in those countries had proved ungrateful for American assistance in the World War. French and British newspapers constantly referred to Uncle Shylock and expressed their conviction that the Americans were ungrateful for the sacrifices they had made in blood and treasure which defended Americans during World War I. In the same vein, however, the French also tried to turn this argument to their advantage both in negotiations and in the press. Did not the Americans comprehend what sacrifices France had made in the name of Western Civilization during the Great War? The Americans might be touchy, but they surely must realize the common interests and common threats which made cooperation a necessity.

France, as Professor Payne so accurately points out, was left with no place else to turn. Britain was a naval power and at least as bankrupt as France through the depredation of war and depression. The Americans must surely see that they alone could stop aggression by aid to their former associated powers. France also tried rapprochement with the Russians, but there seemed less hope for genuine collective security from that quarter because of Russia's inability to provide material aid or technical assistance to the French. Russia might have man power and common enmity with Germany, but the Comintern continued to interfere in French internal affairs which did not breed trust. Most important a treaty with the Russians would not be as significant in threatening Germany as one with the United States whose weight could swing the balance of any war.

Professor Callahan's selection of "Expect Only Words" for his title is ironic for this is precisely the point of view expressed by numerous Americans concerning why the United States should avoid any entangling arrangements with the British or French in the interwar years. Isolationists argued

162

that "Fortress America" was the United State's best defense against aggression and would lead to such a powerful position that no aggressor would dare bother America. Had not the British and French betrayed a sacred trust and fallen to quibbling over debts, reneging on repudiation of secret treaties, and selfishly sought to use the American sacrifice in the Great War to further their own territorial ambitions? Americans of all political perspectives were determined that they would not be used to pull British or other foreign chestnuts from any future fires. Joseph Grew used the phrase concerning chestnuts in describing British policy in Asia, and Franklin Delano Roosevelt avowed that this would not be the purpose of American foreign policy. FDR on more than one occasion said that if the British and French could not act to defend their own interests they should hardly expect the United States to take any initiatives for them.

There is a unifying theme in the essays included in this volume. All three stress the lack of trust and disillusionment which came early or late to each power as it viewed the foreign policy objectives of the others. Professor Callahan looks inside the British economic structure to illustrate that England could not stand alone; England did not really expect to have the American stand with her until Churchill came to power at a time when the feared threats of aggression, unreal until 1939, finally made it feasible to count on Americans acting in self-interest. British statesmen, more accustomed to dealing with the Americans than were either the French or Russians, never had as much faith in words or American perception of long-range interests as the others. More than France or Russia the British understood American pragmatism which shied away from policy planning and action to forestall coming problems. The French and Russians could not believe that foreseeing a threat to their security American leaders would not cooperate to head off the catastrophe. So the illusion of action based on various pronouncements emanating from Washington in the nineteen thirties regularly promoted hope on the part of the continental powers.

Americans failed to understand that the others looked to them because they were the only ones with the economic power and the industrial capacity to force the issue with the

163

arming powers. Not many Americans saw their position as clearly as Edwin L. James of the *New York Times* when he wrote, in October 1930, "America's great world political position is not due primarily to our moral leadership but primarily to our wealth and economic power."* Americans knew that they were a great economic force in the world, but they thought that the world looked to them for moral guidance. Thus, they responded to appeals for aid with sermons which led others to believe they were addled, impotent, selfish, or playing some deeper game that could be fathomed only through constant pinching, prodding, and stirring of the American policy makers. Perhaps the European leaders did not believe in American isolationism because it left them with too bleak a view of their own positions as they attempted to visualize what they could do in the face of world-wide aggression with the numerous and militarily prepared peoples of Germany, Italy, and Japan.

Russia looked askance at the other threatened powers because they were capitalists encircling them and opposing the very survival of the Soviet state. Because the Soviet union was a totalitarian power the Russians could not feel empathy with capitalist-democratic powers. Yet the other totalitarian nations generally also opposed Soviet communism and with the exception of Italy sought Soviet territory. Only the United States among potential enemies was so far removed as to pose no threat to Soviet security, and only the Americans seemed to have mutual interest which could be protected by joint action while possessing the wherewithal to do the job. The common enmity with Japan provided the basis of Soviet hopes for American cooperation plus the communist belief in the inevitability of imperial conflict between the United States and Japan. The mutuality of interest the Russians thought also extended to the German threat but not so directly as to England and France who must see that alliance with Russia was in their own interest in the face of a potential German onslaught. The Soviet leaders thought that England and France had no choice but to align with them,

*Edwin L. James, "Our World Power and Moral Influence," *The International Digest*, I (October, 1930), p. 22.

but the British and French, although they played with the possibility of a cooperative effort with the Russians, did not see this prospect as their primary objective. Russia, after all, was a totalitarian power, not to be trusted to come through when the chips were down. Also, the Soviets had proved themselves self-destructive of their own power with purges which weakened the Red Army to the point that it was unable to stand up very convincingly to the much smaller army of Finland.

These were only further reasons that the British and French found it necessary to search for other answers to their questions concerning how to thwart Axis designs on their power position. Professor Callahan illustrates that the British felt that they could depend on no one but themselves. Thus they tried to solve their security problems in Europe without courting the Americans and were only slightly more convinced that the United States might provide help in Asia. While Neville Chamberlain was Prime Minister, British policy generally aimed at satisfying Hitler and making him feel secure concerning a prominent German position in Central and Eastern Europe while the focus concerning Japan was to bring her to accept a sharing of the Pacific. If this could be done there was hope of recovery for a stable Europe and Asia, with the latter policy stemming from earlier efforts by Stanley Baldwin. British leaders of this period faulted the Americans for not being able to see what they had to do in their own self-interest which was rather like the pot's reference to the kettle. Baldwin and Chamberlain did not ask what they had left if their respective ploys did not work. Professor Callahan does not point out that the Chamberlain policy was based on a one shot proposition at least in part because he was convinced of German invincibility. In Roger Bjerk's dissertation he illustrated the close relationship which developed between Kennedy and Chamberlain and the degree to which they reinforced one another's pessimism concerning the prospects for stopping Hitler in Europe. Kennedy did not visualize the Americans as "safe" from Hitler but thought that at least they had the material resources, personnel, and economic power to prepare for him and that Europe did not. As Wayne Cole has pointed out in his study, this was a position shared by another American who was to influence Chamberlain's thinking, Charles A. Lindbergh. Chamberlain agreed with the Kennedy and Lindbergh assessments of Hitler's power and Britain's weakness. He was also convinced along with Kennedy that there was no alternative to appeasement because the United States would not play a British hand. The main difference between British and French leadership was that Britain found a leader willing to try to turn around their defeatism while the French sunk further in despair as their hopes for assistance from the British and Americans faded.

France held her illusions longer about possible American aid because French leaders knew that Britain would not act without American promises of at least benevolent neutrality and without assistance France was at the mercy of the combined power of Germany and Italy. Russia held her illusions concerning American aid the longest because she felt that the Americans had to recognize that a fight was inevitable and that they needed allies with mutual interests even if they rested on mutual enmities. Russians viewed Americans as ultimate realists who must awaken to the dangers posed to their interests by the Axis powers. Finally the Russians realized that the Americans would not take a leading position unless the European powers did something to show that they were prepared to fight for themselves, and when that hope disappeared with the failure of negotiations between England, France, and Russia in 1939, the Soviets cut loose and made their own appeasement with Hitler. They still did not react with hostility to the Americans, for they blamed the British and French for not making the first move in collective security.

Paralysis of initiative in arming and opposing the aggressors diplomatically has been charged with bringing on World War II. The essays in this volume illustrate some relevance to this thesis based in part on the political timidity of the leaders in England and France. Leadership in all the countries concerned hesitated to place before their peoples the realities which all came to perceive concerning threats posed by the aggressively inclined nations to their security and world-wide trade or territorial interests. Russia was the only one of the future

166

allies which in any way prepared its population for a possible war, but Soviet leaders led them to think of the whole world as enemies. They created confusion and a morale breakdown in the Russian people's response to the war by their own propaganda, switching from collective security to appeasement and back to collective security after the Nazi attack. Russia was, however, still more prepared militarily and psychologically than her two World War I major European allies. French leadership felt betrayed and alone, and these men passed on their defeatism to their people. They put faith in the Maginot Line which they did not wholeheartedly believe would work, and they blamed England directly and the Americans indirectly for the failure to insure the maintenance of the Versailles settlement.

If there is a valid criticism of the Payne and Callahan articles it is their adoption of the arguments of the countries they examined relative to the blame each placed on the United States for the failure of collective security and for the foundation of a lack of trust resting on American perfidy and/or blindness to American interests. While it is true that FDR and Secretary of State Cordell Hull were lacking in the qualities of firm leadership in the face of what FDR especially saw as real threats emanating from Germany and Japan, it must be admitted that timid American efforts at cooperation were not enthusiastically greeted by French and British leaders. They demanded firmer commitments. The words of Maxim Litvinov provide an accurate assessment of the roles played by these men: "In the great trans-atlantic republic isolationism has made such great headway that one can hardly reckon on its eventual cooperation, particularly if in Europe itself there is not formed beforehand a firmly welded group opposing aggression with an appreciable chance of success." (Degra, *Soviet Documents*, III, 290.) There was no such cooperation in Europe. Instead many eyes were turned westward searching for a fair wind from the United States which would blow away the gathering storm clouds, and though the wind finally came it was too late to prevent the clouds from first raining a devastating destruction over all of Europe for six long years.

167

170

171

172